Oh Don!

By John Sammon

Prologue

The election of Donald Trump devastated me.

I never liked Hillary Clinton and I didn't like her husband when he was president and I didn't want a former first lady to become president; one Clinton in the White House was enough and it was time to move on I thought-----but Trump was so much worse.

I did not vote for either Clinton or Trump although in retrospect I might have voted for Clinton just to try and stop Trump. Withholding a vote boycotting a candidate because you refuse to vote for the lesser of two evils is a kind of vote, and I disagree with people who say if you didn't vote don't complain. I didn't vote and my non-vote was a complaint against a lack of decent candidates.

However as bad as Clinton is or was, Trump was worse far worse than anyone I've ever seen. I've never seen anything like Trump before. This has nothing to do with political viewpoint.

The election of Donald Trump badly shook my faith in the American people about 45 percent of them, and in the U.S. Constitution, which despite safeguards put in by the founders could not prevent the first really bad man from becoming president.

The single most frightening development is the rise in supporters, supposedly reasonable intelligent people of any party, who refuse to criticize elected representatives of their own party for anything and particularly the president, no matter what they do wrong. This blind faith (often exhibited by young people), is the single gravest threat to a representative form of government in which basic ethics means survival.

Trump's candidacy was like no other.

As far as my memory goes back and I have been following politics since the 1960's I could not recall a candidate who insulted other candidates with such reckless abandon over their looks, their gender, their whatever, also fixing vicious demeaning labels on them (Little Marco), as did Donald Trump.

I could not recall sadistic political rallies where Trump led cheers among followers some of whom seemed to be almost foaming at the mouth as they taunted in one example a young black girl. Trump called for another protester to be physically beaten and carried out on a stretcher.

The only small similarity I could recall was the ill-fated presidential bid of George Wallace in 1968, an avowed racist and as usual with anything regarding Trump-----Trump's campaign was worse. Even Richard Nixon with his lies and cynical, ugly, behind-the-scenes obscene smears against opponents could demonstrate at times human impulses and a sense of wit and humor.

Trump has no humor. Trump scowls. Trump insults. Trump tweets. That's about it.

America has always been a country of haters in addition to what is good about this country, a country of the Ku Klux Klan, and millions more who are benign racists. They don't burn crosses on your lawn but they don't think you're as good as they are if your skin is of a different color. They deny they are racist.

The election of Donald Trump was an attempt to turn back the clock to 1958 by mostly angry white people who felt they had been ignored and abused and so voted for a man with no experience in government service but who promised them glory and riches if they did. These are people who believed and said out loud that the system was broken.

However, they were usually unable to specify exactly how the system was broken, or how electing a man who has made a career out of trading and selling properties and gambling casinos would fix the break---other than his own promises. Revenge, a chance to get even with whoever, seemed to be the sentiment behind the election of Trump.

I wrote this book "Oh Don" because I felt such pain at the election of someone who stands for everything I despise in a human being. I couldn't just sit as a hapless, helpless spectator---or victim might be more appropriate. I value honesty; Trump is a serial liar (during a debate 58 percent compared to Clinton's 18 percent). I value humility; Trump is a braggart and a bully. I served in the military, Trump did not.

I don't mock and grope women---Trump did and does.

I felt I had to do something that would oppose this behavior. I couldn't just wait for the next election in four years and hope for the best.

I felt I could challenge someone whose power makes him similar to a god in my own small way as a so-called "average citizen," by using my writing skills to shame and mock Trump for his continuing lack of integrity. But it would be done in a way that would humorously encourage him to change his ways.

I knew this was unlikely, as a leopard can't change his spots as they say. Trump's inappropriate behavior at least in his mind is responsible for his imagined past success collecting and investing other people's money.

If I could speak to Trump in the most simple way possible free of political or policy complexities that would only divert the basic message-----If I could talk to Donald Trump as though I were a child with a child's total honesty and a child's total lack of fear, hate, envy, malice, jealousy----the pure uncorrupted mind of a child.

I could use a truth so brutally honest it would be hard to counter for example with statistics, distorted facts and figures or smokescreens.

To do this I would need to talk directly to Trump as though I was writing him a letter.

Rather than belittle him only I would tell him in these letters how he could become a better person. Trump himself publicly said he would 'try" to become a better person during the election campaign and the furor when he was caught on tape saying he could grab a woman's genitals because he was a star.

That's what "Oh Don" is about, me giving Trump advice, giving him a way out, a way to do better if he will just change. I know it's probably hopeless.

Of the 34 advice columns in the book I doubt Trump has seen any of them even though I posted them on his Facebook page. Someone always erases them quickly after I post them (one time two Arabs in the Middle East hit the "Like" button on their computers before my piece on Trump's Facebook page was erased).

This is not a book about political philosophy or who is right, right or left. I can respect a person with whom I disagree politically if they give me a reason to respect them. This is instead a book for anyone who wants Trump to act presidential-------instead of what we have.

John Sammon

Now Don!

2-20-2017

This is another one of my open letters to Don Trump and as before, I'm not going to call you Donald because that is the name of a duck, nor am I going to call you "The Donald," because that's stupid that's showing off, and you've done enough of that.

That's like me calling myself Master Jonathan.

Bull!

Now Don, I said when you took office I was going to do my best if not to try and like you then at least tolerate you for four years, but you're making it extremely difficult for me. Once again as I said before, you don't know me and to you I'm a loser because unlike you I didn't inherit millions from my father and use it to talk other people out of their money and avoid paying taxes which you call patriotic and one reason why you won't release your tax forms.

You don't want me to find out.

We could also see your dealings with the Russians, but that's another story and I won't waste space.

First of all, stop smirking. Now write it on the blackboard Don 300 times...I will not smirk...I will not smirk.

You see, when you smirk it makes me want to hate your guts. And you said you were going to unite people. I don't want that to join your other lies that amount to about 85 percent of all the things you say.

Get a picture of Jesus Christ. In all the representations of Christ (and no he doesn't look like you or a blonde Brad Pitt), in all those pictures, have you ever seen Christ smirk? No. Not at all. Not once. Christ looks like he is suffering. Christ looks earnest, which builds empathy.

Why can't you look this way Don? Your other panoply of looks, anger, mockery, rolling your eyes in a malicious way, are the real you, but unless you want more than just rednecks and haters to respect you, you must practice something that is foreign to your nature…..integrity….and humility.

Now go to the bathroom mirror Don and practice looking ernest. In case you don't know what that word means, it means having depth, seriousness and genuineness, instead of shallow, mocking, snarling and petty.

I know these are hard to learn. But you can learn, one way is to read one of Mark Twain's masterpieces (ie. Connecticut Yankee and Tom Sawyer), which often dealt with issues of integrity, courage and the opposite, being a phony.

You see Don if you want people to be enthusiastic about you and your policies you have to reach beyond just appealing to haters who want to get revenge on the country for what they believe is its exclusion of them, you know, many of them white guys who resent blacks, gays, uppity women (Rosie O'Donnell), immigrants and the rest.

Don, you can't fragment the country into winners and losers if you want to get anything done and using the media as a scapegoat by whipping up hatred against a free press that asks you impertinent and sometime inconvenient questions. Don, Don, Don! You have to rise above it.

Let me give you an example. Abraham Lincoln has gone down in history as our greatest president. I won't go over his achievements except to say that a cabinet official who once called him a "Baboon" Lincoln still appointed to high office because the official was the best person for the job and Lincoln knew this and was able to rise above petty spite. If it was you Don you'd call the guy a "Waste of skin" and insult his wife as a "Fat Cow" for good measure.

Don't do it Don. Don't! The more the media and Saturday Night Live pick on you and the more you take it with generosity, the more the public will develop some sympathy and support for you.

You have to understand Don what up until now has been a foreign concept for you, that the measure of a man is not how much he can parade around and act the big guy and boast and taunt and make faces. The measure of a man comes from quiet resolve and restraint. Look at your own VP Pence. I don't like his policies but I can at least listen to him.

I'm not gonna listen to you not unless you change. We don't have to be a divided and mean-spirited country Don. Not if you will reject it. The issue is up to you. It's in your chair.

Now Don, Calm Down

2-23-2017

Now Don, I'm not going to call you Donald, because that's the name of a duck, and I'm not going to call you "The Donald," because why say in two words what you can say in one unless you're an egomaniac who always thinks more of anything is better.

For example, more sex (not better sex), more money (not more charity donations one reason of five why you hide your taxes), or more ego (there's never enough of that is there Don?)
Besides, do I call my wife "The wife?"

Now Don, you recently flew into a rage in front of family members and demagogue philosophical inquisitor advisors in the Oval Office (you literally blew your top), and Don, maybe this isn't the job for you.

A man who can't control his temper with his finger on the nuclear trigger? One of the prerequisites for being a president is to remain calm in a crisis. You think that trying to hide your Russian involvement by doing a smokescreen accusing Obama of wiretaps is a crisis? As they said in show business, "You ain't seen nuthin' yet."

This is a tempest in a teapot Don.

Now repeat after me Don, when you feel like knocking someone's teeth down their throat, when you feel threatened and that ever-moist sense of self-pity urge tugs at you, repeat after me Don, "Everybody is not out to get me, everybody is not out to get me. Repeat this 100 times. Now, Don, take deep breaths.

You see Don, if you get angry like this in only your first month when something really bad happens you're going to have a heart attack.

I can only guess what you said to your Chief of Staff Reince Priebus (would you trust a guy named Reince?) Evidently, his parents didn't know how to spell "Prince." And Steve Bannon, the right wing combined equivalent of Rasputin and Andre Vyshinsky, head prosecutor and dungeon master for Joe Stalin at the 1930's show trials (they believed in alternative facts too Don).

Though the transcripts have yet to be made public, when Attorney General Jeff Sessions forgot and slipped and caught himself being honest by recusing himself from the investigation into your alleged ties with your Russian buddies in the Kremlin, Don, you said something to the effect of, "Goddamn mother....' (obscenity deleted but usually associated with a pleasant form of procreation).

Then Don, you most likely said swear words some of us have never even heard of before like *%@(^^#@))(^^$#$(&%^^&!!!!!

Is this any way for the leader of the free world to act Don? Or is it the behavior of a selfish, spoiled, petty, malicious, cowardly, whining, self-pitying two-bit punk in a pin-striped suit.

Let's assume for argument's sake Obama was wiretapping you because of your Russian dealings. As we all know from the O.J. Simpson case it's going to be hard to prove, everything is always hard to prove. Almost always every investigation goes nowhere, results in nothing. There is almost always no smoking gun.

You're the president not Obama. So why bring it up? Why create another crisis (mini petty) though it may be, for no good reason? Nothing that's going to pay you political dividends, all its done is to intensify interest in your Russian adventures. With all that you're facing, for example, a North Korean missile hitting Seattle, why needless stir the brown stuff floating in the toilet?

That is..............unless there's something really bad you've done and need to hide. Something you're really desperate to keep secret. A person would have to be pretty riled up to make such an outlandish claim.

Now Don, when somebody loses control of themselves it's bad. When the president does it it's worse (remember when Nixon slapped around Ron Ziegler the Press Secretary because Nixon was angry at the media)?

Also, when you make an issue of how Arnold the weightlifter screwed up your TV game show it makes me doubt your sanity Don.

I want you to get and read a copy of my soon-to-be-released book, "How to Act Presidential if you're a Dummy…..Beyond a Mere Scripted Speech to Congress." The book will give you advice on how you can act like you have integrity and courage even if you don't. There are also chapters on maintaining composure, giving off a feeling of warmth when you secretly despise most people, and most importantly, how to act like you know what you're doing rather than a guy who is not up to the job and who regardless of politics, is in over his head.

Now Don….Now That You're Scapegoating Reporters

2-28-2017

Now Don, I'm not going to call you Donald because that's the name of a duck, and I'm not going to call you "The Donald," because nobody in their right mind would call you that unless they have a fetish, get a hard-on by getting into improper word syntax.

Besides you're not a "The," anyway, and you're certainly not an "It" (some people think you're a "Thing")…Instead you're a "You!" Or a "Me!" Use a personal pronoun.

Which brings to mind…One of your supporters who didn't like my opinion recently called me a loser in an email and also called me one of "You people." He said something like, "You people do this and this and this (like many conservatives he wants to try and demonize anyone of the other party, in a system that has run this country pretty well using two parties both composed mostly of loyal Americans since 1790).

Anyway, I corrected this Bozo by telling him he was "Freudian slipping" (giving away his neurosis) in two ways. First of all, I told him and I'll tell you Don….there are no winners and losers……there are only people.

And it's not "You people"…. it's "Us people."

We both get up in the morning Don you and I, and we both yawn and possibly belch and scratch our heads and walk to the bathroom. We both relieve ourselves to the sound of disgusting bodily functions. My toilet is made of white porcelain while yours is made of gold plate no doubt. Now Don, if you want to think that makes you a winner go right ahead and think that.

When you die you won't take that gold toilet with you, which brings us to reporters.

Reporters are just people like all the rest of us Don, except their business is asking questions that often the person being questioned if he or she is a political officeholder find…how can I say it…inconvenient…or unpleasant? This is especially true if the political officeholder has a lot of controversial things to explain.

Remember the old saying Don, "There are three things on which people can't agree….how to make love, how to stoke the fireplace fire and how to run a newspaper." It should be updated now to say, "There are three things upon which right-wing nut jobs and sycophant slave fans of yours can agree….that news people are "Leftist…Leftist…Leftist!"

Use of the term "Leftist" is deliberate because Don, "Leftist" rhymes with "Communist," and seems more evil than the word "Democrat," which rhymes with democracy, which has a rather pleasant connotation.

Now Don, some reporters are Democrats. They have a right to be. It's a free country with a Constitution that guarantees the right to disagree (hopefully without being accused of disloyalty) in a two-party system.

Don, how come the private political preference of reporters is so much an obsession of yours and not that of plumbers? Plumbers are a group. They're important too. They come out and fix your drainpipe. You don't care what party they belong to, do you?

Nobody cares what a plumber believes.

Now Don, look, I know you want to cast reporters as a scapegoat in the same way Hitler did the Jews, to take people's minds off your performance (or lack of) and to come up with a whipping boy you can always depend on to throw your supporters into a blood-lust feeding frenzy of hate and desire for revenge and worship of you. Accusations of disloyalty worked in the Joe McCarthy Red Scare days and it still does today.

I know you'll try and disagree with this at first, but Don, most reporters (and I've been one) are decent people and not Machiavellian schemers, most of them try to be fair, just like most people are decent, and most Democrats believe it or not are also decent people who simply disagree on how best to run the country.

Truly evil people out to destroy the system are rare….unless you want to create a false sense of peril….use fear and hate…for some political reason. Don, you're not like that. C'mon!

I might advise you Don to keep on baiting the media if I thought scapegoating them as "Enemies of the People" would work forever. But the problem Don is….How can I tell you this? You reach a point of diminishing returns Don, where it gets old, hearing the same thing over and over like an old scratchy song record.

And you've got maybe a long way to go Don.

When the public finally gets tired of hearing it, who you gonna blame then?

If everything goes well, no wars, good economy, everybody rich, everybody happy, it won't matter what reporters say will it Don? It's only when things are rotten Don you need to scapegoat a group to divert attention.

Right Don? I will use Anne Frank's quote, "Despite everything, I believe people are really good at heart."

Please Don, don't scapegoat.

Now Don...How Many Times....Have I told Ya'...?

2-30-2017

Here's another open letter to Don Trump. I won't call you Donald because that's the name of a duck, and I won't call you The Donald, because that's you trying to act like a bigshot but instead it's just stupid.

Do we call Bozo the Clown "The Bozo?" Do we call actor Brad Pitt "The Pitt?" Do I call myself "The Sammon?"

Even God we don't call, "The God."

What makes you so special, Don?

This is improper English language usage anyway and you've already been slaughtering the English language Don. You used the word "braggadocious" (means to brag) which is ironic in two ways. You were trying to make out you weren't bragging about something when in truth you brag about almost everything (including the size of your penis). What's even stranger is "braggadocioous" is an old English word from the 19th century that hasn't been used in 100 years.

Are you going to give us a speech in old English saying "Forsooth, take ye heed yon varlet (means jerk), for thou hast my dander up, are thee and thy also braggadocious?"

Don! You've been sitting in a skyscraper in Manhattan too long Don. You need to join the real world and get real. I'm here to help you Don.

I'm going to show you how you can survive and avoid impeachment and all the agony and mess you are certainly headed for. Your poll numbers are dropping faster than a North Korean test missile. I'm your unofficial advisor. I'm here to save you from ruin.

Let's talk taxes, or tax returns to be more exact.

I know you're sitting there in the White House saying to yourself, "I hate this job already. Gee I miss New York."

You just received a petition signed by a million people demanding that you make public your tax returns. Here's what we do. Take the petition, open your desk drawer and place the petition inside. Shut the drawer.

Now repeat after me, "I don't see a petition. Do you see a petition? What petition?"

What would the revealing of your tax returns do for the public, a bunch of do-gooder busybodies, anyway?

Okay, so it would show that you don't have as much money as you claimed. So what? Big deal! Everybody wants more money than they really have. What's wrong with that? That's just being an American. It's even patriotic.

And okay, so your tax returns will show you didn't pay any taxes. That's okay too, you're just smarter than the rest of us like you say, we're all a bunch of suckers and losers who support a system you've figured a legal way (loopholes) to take advantage of. Taking advantage, what could be more American?

Yes and the returns will show you didn't donate to charities like you said. A bunch of leeches, there will always be losers who need free money.

Yeah and okay, so your tax returns will show you've had some secret business dealings with the Russians. This is only common sense. We don't want trouble with a big country like Russia or China. We only fight small impoverished countries like Iraq and then brag how tough we are. Tell people you've been working behind the scenes (in secret) to make our relations with Russia friendlier, and at the same time taking the Russians for oodles of rubles, their own money. If the Russians want to let you (obscenity deleted) do it to them and pay you for the privilege, what's wrong with that?

Wasn't this The Art of the Deal, as in the title of your book, where you made an art-form like a Picasso masterpiece out of fast-talking someone out of their ill-gotten gains? Where's the appreciation for your genius?

It's no different than when you hire an American contractor to do a job on one of your casinos and then when he's finished refuse to pay for the job and when he complains threaten him by saying, "Try and sue me I have 100 lawyers and I can outspend you in court. I can bankrupt you!"

The contractor always goes away unpaid. It's the same with the Russians. They're a deep pocket. The public and the liberal media are a bunch of ingrates. They don't understand how much you've suffered using the Russians to your and our own benefit.

So the Russians gave you some gifts, including a thousand pounds of caviar and vodka to wash it down with and a promise to introduce you for a good time to a wild Russian girl named Oxana. So what? Did you take that gift?

Yes you did, but not Oxana. Next to her name you scribbled "Not yet we'll see."

That is not a conflict of interest.

Do the American people appreciate your sacrifice? Hell no!

Okay, you had some business dealings with the Mafia. That's your business and nobody else's. John F. Kennedy slept with a mob boss's girlfriend and the liberal media loved him.

Besides, nobody's perfect!

Always remember one thing Don. If you believe in it....it's not a lie.

Sooooo Big!

3-2-2017

Now Don, I'm not going to call you Donald, because that's the name of a duck, and I'm not going to call you "The Donald," because that was a way ancient morons of nobility used to call themselves so they could feel like bigshots; for example, Otto The Feeble of Saxony, and Pliny The Elder, who got buried by Mt. Vesuvius in 79. That's pretty dumb, rushing off toward an eruption.

To act even bigger should they have called themselves instead "The Feeble," or "The Pliny?"

Now Don, that speech to Congress, was that the real you? Or was it the act of a chameleon? Not once during the address did you call Rosie O'Donnell a fat pig as you have in the past, not once did you mimic the speech impediment of a reporter, or call John McCain senile.

I'm proud of you Don.

The only potential problem is how long will the new more likeable you hold? Three days? You might be a Jekyll and Hyde, you know, drink the potion and flip out. You can control a speech and I have a suspicion that as soon as the brief afterglow wears off you'll revert to the old you, always blaming others and never taking responsibility for anything when it's bad. For example when you said you had the biggest electoral college win since Ronald Reagan and this was immediately pointed out as a lie (not an alternative fact); you blamed an aide, saying "Someone else told me that."

I hope you can learn and I'm willing to give you the chance.

Even though you behaved yourself during the speech and didn't act like no one in American political history has ever acted before (your supporters think rudeness is cool), during the speech you made some really disturbing comments. For example, remember back during the campaign when you said, "I'm going to make the military soooooo big, nobody will dare mess with us."

"Sooooooo big?"

Who talks like that Don? I've never heard anyone talk this way. Do I go around telling the clerk at the grocery store, "Just put my bottle of wine in the bag waaaaayyyy down?" The clerk would think I was an escapee from a mental ward, and he'd be right to think so.

Two major mistakes Don. You want to build up our nuclear arsenal when we can already destroy the world ten times over. This will result in an arms race and Don, you didn't learn from as far back as World War I that an arms race doesn't make the world a safer place. Learn from World War I Don. You know what World War I was, right? It's something bad that happened 100 years ago.

The second mistake is that no mention was made of the fiscal cost of increasing the size of the military as you like to put it "Soooooooooo big!" Weapons systems cost a lot of money and Ronald Reagan already made the mistake of military spending like there was no tomorrow and put this country further into the red (debt) several times over.

Republicans always make the same mistake (Bush did too). They talk about smaller government and then military spend like a (pardon the pun) drunken sailor.

Maintenance of a lean and effective strike force capability and working closely with allies is more reasonable than overkill wasteful weapons systems and the accompanying boastful ravings of military might and grandeur similar to that of a kid squealing with delight while playing with a toy battleship in the bathtub.

Instead of being specific on how you will pay for what will be an enormous sum, instead vague references were made to collecting unpaid taxes (including your own, Don?); raising a spending cap (borrowing more from China is always good), cracking down on welfare fraud (that might purchase one modern battle tank), and fees from increased energy production.

Really Don, you gonna punish oil companies and their drilling with your plans for a super army?

As one observer understatedly and sardonically put it, "Trump undercut his proposals by soft pedaling the cost."

Which brings us to vainglory and reality, or the lack of reality; vainglory in the dictionary is defined as "excessive vanity."

Excessive vanity?

Don could this be you? The man who before a group of veterans who had won the Congressional Medal of Honor (you often have to die to win one), said "I'm brave too."

Lack of reality speaks for itself.

Don, you haven't learned. I want you to get a book and study Lyndon Johnson. He tried to fight the war in Vietnam and at the same time cure poverty in the country with expenditures, and, as worthy as a part of this was, it just wasn't realistic. Johnson accomplished neither victory in Vietnam nor over poverty and died a broken man.

There's always a cost Don. It's also called Murphy's Law.

It's easiest to promise things Don.

Lying is now the Job

3-17-2017

I have a question for all you right wing fanatics out there, you know, the kind who if Trump went down to a grocery store and held it up at gunpoint….you'd say it's okay. Or ignore it.

Oh, I know what you'd say, the classic Two Wrongs Make a Right Smokescreen Dodge.

You'd say, "Hillary (or Obama) did it too" (held up a store at gunpoint).

I've heard this excuse so many times I've lost count. However, this is not a political philosophy right versus left issue….but one of simple ethics. Let me ask another question. If you are a right winger and this can apply to those who consider themselves to be liberals too. Have you ever once, just once, criticized an elected representative of your own party? For anything? Just once?

Don't lie. It's a "yes" or "no" answer and don't give me the bullsh't (alternative fact), "Well the other guys (opposition party) do it too."

If the answer is no, and we know with many of you it is, you are not only not a good citizen always complaining about how government hasn't properly represented you, but never calling members of your own party on their wrongdoing.

Perhaps you agree with wrongdoing and call it righteousness.

I personally believe you should be more critical of your own party because according to you they represent you and they should stand for what's right. Right?

Are you a small part of a vast conspiracy now led by Trump to legitimize and institutionalize lying as part of the job of the presidency?

Now Don, I won't call you Donald, because that's the name of a duck, and I won't call you "The Donald," because Easter is coming and New Mexico Governor Lew Wallace titled his book "Ben-Hur, A Tale of the Christ."

The Donald? The Christ?

Are you comparing yourself to Christ Don?

On that note before we start we all remember that Don went before a group of veterans who had won the Congressional Medal of Honor our nation's highest military decoration (you often have to die to win one), and told them, "You know, I'm brave too."

If Jesus came into a room and Trump was there he would walk over to Christ and say, "I heard about you and that cross gig...you know....I've suffered too."

Where was I?

Oh yes, the president lying and it's okay with you (the Trump fanatic).

After all, Democrats lie too don't they? So it's okay. You don't hold your own party to a higher standard of conduct and the reason you don't is you want to believe........you have to believe in whatever......Trump will make me happy.........Trump will make me rich........Trump will turn America back into 1958 when blacks and women knew their place.

Now Don, you said your inauguration had one of the biggest crowds in history and that was a lie (aerial photos clearly showed otherwise). You call it an alternative fact. I call it "Bullshi.'t." That's okay with your supporters.

Stop lying Don.

What about a president who lies by telling lies and then lies that he doesn't lie. One way is to make accusing statements without supporting evidence. If for example I called you a child molester and I didn't have any evidence to back it up, you wouldn't like it.

Don said during the campaign that if he shot somebody with a pistol you'd still vote for him? Is this literally true?

Maybe it is in your case.

But it lacks facts, so at best it's conjecture, at worst it's a lie. Don't lie Don.

Oh I know Obama said a similar thing that if he chopped your head off with an axe, you'd still vote for him. So that makes it all okay.

I've never been a Democrat by the way.

I'm just a person who values truth.

Trump attempts to mask lies by saying things like, "I didn't mean literally if I shot someone, just figuratively."

This form of lying, by inference or symbolic-figure-of-speech, he did again last week when his mouthpiece (Spicer) said Trump didn't "literally" mean Obama had wiretapped his ivory tower headquarters during the election. He just meant that Obama had done other nefarious snooping things (Spicer as always didn't specify exactly what).

It may turn out that Obama did something. That's not the point here.

This is a new technique of lying. It's akin to what Reagan once called "Plausible deniability" (don't tell me how you carry out my illegal assignment so I can lie I didn't know anything about it).

You leave yourself an opening to retreat if the public outrage over a bald-faced lie pins you down. Thus, you say, "I didn't mean that in the real sense, I just meant it in general terms."

It's still "Bullsh.t."

Don, you are the first president in U.S. History who believes using a lie to attack perceived enemies and to further your cause is not just an occasional isolated tactical way to get something you want. You believe it to be a continuing standard-operating-procedure part of the job itself, as routine as sharpening a pencil at your desk.

This has never happened before in the office. Earlier liars, Nixon, Johnson, Clinton, resorted to lying only when they felt they had to. You Don! You lie as a matter of basic job skills. To deflect attention from the uncomfortable, to damage opponents (Nixon did this one), to further the image you are decisive and for other reasons.

You gave it away years ago Don when you said in a Freudian slip, something like, "If I didn't stand up to (bully) people, they would mock me."

I think you lie Don because you're afraid not to.

That must be the truth, isn't it Don?

Don't lie Don. It will be the ruin of you.

Oh Don, Learning to Keep Your Mouth Shut

3-23-2017

Oh Don, I won't call you "Donald," because that's the name of a duck, and I won't call you "The Donald," because for some reason it reminds me of "Vlad the Impaler," you know, Count Dracula, perhaps also because Vlad is the first name of your Kremlin buddy Putin.

Now Don, as we move into week nine of your presidency and I'm proud of you because it's been a straight five days since you've done anything really stupid, I want to first have a little talk with you about your disturbing habit of saying anything you please----or in other words, shooting off that enormous mouth of yours.

Before we do that, why do your supporters support everything you do? There's this Facebook webpage of fanatics in Las Vegas (this is fitting the gambling capital they gambled on a megalomaniac to be president), and all their opinions target only the opposition party. They never I mean never criticize a member of their own party and never never you Don. You're lucky in that way Don. You've got a base of support unburdened by logic.

That means that if you went down to a grocery store and held it up at gunpoint it would be alright with them. They'd either A – Say it didn't happen, B – Turn a blind eye, C – Say the store deserved to be held up.

A woman on this right wing Sin City page said Don you were a "Real Man." This is apparently the extent of her total based-on-scientific-thought-and-extensive-investigatory-assessment endorsement of you. But it begs the question, what is a real man, and what is an imitation man? All of us as men are born with a male sexual organ. I look down at mine just like Don does his.

Mine also rises (to quote Hemingway), so does Don's.

Is it because she's slavish and like a dog wants a master, a he-man? Is she into S & M, B & D, R & O?

I can't be certain because this woman's "Real Man" statement is so obtuse, but if I had to venture a guess, it might be to reason that to her, your bluntness, rudeness, bragging, pompous swaggering, mocking, insulting, serial lying and personal threats against those who disagree with you (you said you would destroy the career of one), she equates with a curious kind of decisive and wise, no-nonsense leadership.

Another woman on this (to the right of Genghis Khan) web page said, "We've had eight years of the other." This is a blanket endorsement of you Don. That means it applies to everybody and everything in a one-size-fits-all condemnation. In other words, there are no honest members of government (the other party). They're all dishonest, not just the former president who I suspect she didn't like among other reasons in that he has a dark skin. I won't demonize a person who disagrees with me like they do and will give her the benefit of the doubt that this isn't the case.

All members of government (the other party) are dishonest and none not one wants the best for the country. None of them are simply exercising their right to be wrong under the Constitution. They're all evil conspirators in a subversive plot.

What she really wants is not a two-party system with the right to disagree where we still value each other as Americans of the kind that has led this country for over 200 years. What she wants is one-party autocracy.

How better than to cure the evil of big government dishonesty among the elite than by electing a guy who acts like Henry VIII and is a gambling king-pin renowned for his shady business deals, for example, hiring small contractors to do work on his casino and then not paying them and when they complain threatening to take them to court and out-spend them into bankruptcy with attorney fees.

It all makes sense to me. Don to your supporter you're a Washington "Outsider." In this case it means you're an octopus like the dishonest (other party) bureaucrat, but just one of a different color. Or in other words, you cure dishonesty in government by electing a dishonest man with no experience in government who claims he's honest.

Again it makes sense.

Okay moving on. Where were we? You're big mouth Don. In the old days, in your ivory tower penthouse with its thousand-dollar-bill toilet paper, you could order me to "Jump!" I would have to say, "How high?" Those days are over Don. You used to just snap your finger, but that's over.

Now you have to be accountable, Don.

The next time you feel the urge to accuse someone or something without proof, and then make it all worse by accusing a foreign country of being in on the scheme, again without proof, straining relations with that foreign country for no good reason. Go to the mirror and say, "The next time I need to I will keep my big mouth shut!"

Repeat it 50 times.

Don't blame Spicer, the albino (he's so white he glows in the dark), who imitates the actress Melissa McCarthy on Saturday Night live. He's just a flunky.

Now Don, That's Strike Two

4-4-2017

Now Don, I won't call you Donald because that's the name of a duck, and I won't call you "The Donald," because when you come to the Danube River you don't say "Hi Danube!" The Danube River is a thing, not a person you say, "There's the Danube."

If I say "The Donald," it means you're a thing not a person, like the river is a thing. Are you a thing Don?

Now Don, the first few months have been rough. We had that Muslim ban and the courts stopped it and then we had your replacement for Obama Health Care and your own extremists didn't like that and that went south too. And the Mexican Wall, well, that' doesn't seem to be going anywhere either.

As they say in baseball, you're zero for two Don. There's only one advantage so far. I don't see how you can keep going hitless (avoid achieving something).

It can only go up from here, right?

It's a funny thing. The people who elected you Don voted for you because you are an "Outsider," someone with no government experience. Let's use logic here. When you need a plumber, do you search for someone who has never worked as a plumber, who has never fixed a pipe? When you want to fly in a plane do you go out to the airport and search for someone who has never piloted a plane and say, "Take me up?"

No, you don't do that.

When you want your car worked on do you find someone who doesn't know what a wrench is?

No!

Yet the most powerful position in the history of the world, they want someone who has no background in it at all. It's a paradox.

The other reason people voted for you is that they believe you will run government like a business. You'll make them all rich. Let's go back to logic. Is government a business? In a business you have a private enterprise run primarily for profit. A government represents constituents and is assigned with the wellbeing of the public as a whole, a different animal completely.

Let me put it another way. Do you run a train locomotive in the same way as a sailboat? They both move forward. A train runs on a track and burns gas or coal or electric power and a sailboat is run at the caprice of the winds. They're different. If you know how to run one you don't know how to run the other.

You can't run government strictly like a business.

Don, you yourself have already proven that government is not a business. When you make policy changes, judges challenge it, when you try to deport immigrants, cities sue you. It's not like the old days when you sat in a skyscraper tower and a flunky came into your office and you snapped your finger and they jumped.

Unlike a private business, democracy or a republic is a participatory, populist and consensus exercise involving other people----not just you Don. You're going to have to change your attitude if you're going to survive. First of all, you need someone to give you advice and listen to it. The idea that you're smart enough to fly the airplane without learning how first is not going to work.

Find someone to advise you who is a realist and not a politically philosophical demagogue. Bannon is as useless to you as a turtle flipped on its back. The idea that I know everything or I don't need to know anything I don't already know---you won't survive your first term Don.

Where do we go from here? First of all, Don, would you quit acting so guilty about your involvement with the Russians, always freaking out and sending tweets like you're doing a smokescreen? I remember Watergate Don and how it just kept going on and on and getting in deeper and deeper in the (human excrement) for Nixon until he was forced to resign----and you sure act like you've got something to hide Don.

Instead, tell the media, "I look forward to an impartial and independent investigation because I am innocent of any wrongdoing and they can look into whatever they want."

Practice saying this over and over 300 times Don.

Oh Don, Welcome to War

4-9-2017

The Russians learned a painful lesson. You can't trust Don Trump.

Oh Don, I'm not going to call you Donald, because that's the name of a duck, and I'm not going to call you "The Donald," because the syntax is wrong and many of your fanatic followers like to slaughter the English language like the one who called me an (expletive deleted but means the rectal orifice), by saying, "UR an (expletive deleted)."

With UR she meant the word "You're."

Let's start out here first by saying, don't get me wrong Don. I approve of the bombing of Syria to get back at the no-good bastards for the chemical gas attack and a response, any kind of strong response, is called for. See Don as well as being your unofficial advisor I'm a fair man. If you do something right I'll give you credit.

I said from the very start of this weekly "Oh Don" column that if you would stop cheating, lying, grabbing womens' behinds without their permission, bragging, posing, insulting, mocking physical impediments on people and the weight of fat women----and all the rest.

If you do what's right I'll support it.

I knew that when you took office a war would result soon, but you still continue to be the "President of Irony," Don. The Russians, who helped elect you and who wanted you to win the presidency and who computer hacked the Democrat Headquarters (no need for a Watergate break-in), the Russians, who wanted no part of Hillary Clinton.

You double-crossed the Russians Don. Good boy!

Putin is sitting there in the Kremlin saying to himself, "You think you know a guy and what does he go and do? After all we've done to help him. He wouldn't be there (White House) if it wasn't for us...for me rather. I made you who you are today. If it wasn't for me you'd still be a TV game show host."

I'm loving it Don, good call.

Now then, we all know that a war is on the threshold, probably either in Syria or North Korea or both. The likelihood of war with Russia isn't very likely because the major powers-that-be (Russia, China, U.S.) have a healthy wariness of each other and want to preserve their options to rule the world by means other than a nuclear catastrophe.

It's North Korea with its bubble boy marshmallow head and that Stalinist puppet gas-bag in Damascus we have to worry about and in the case of North Korea it's not "If," just "When." They're not going to give up targeting the U.S. West Coast with a missile and we can't let them do it.

Here's another irony Don. People voted for you because you have no past experience in government when the same people wouldn't hire a plumber to fix their pipe with no prior experience. People voted for you because they think you'll run the government like a business even though this is lunacy----government isn't a business.

Businesses don't declare war Don.

The ultimate irony is perhaps that you will order soldiers into combat and you are a draft dodger who skipped and made money while I was serving on a front line. You are soon going to order soldiers into harm's way when you yourself would never have gone there. It isn't a requirement to serve, but one who never did and suddenly becomes Commander in Chief, it's a bit ironic wouldn't you say?

I won't hold it against you if you act wisely.

Here are some tips Don and mistakes to avoid if we can learn from the past and its mistakes. Don't fight a winless war where you (and we) fail to go all out to win a quick and decisive decision. No Vietnam-like war that drags on and on endlessly and where we impose constraints on ourselves that make a decisive decision all but impossible (in Vietnam we hoped bombing would force them to give up).

Either fight to win or get out Don.

Americans will support action you order in the beginning and then the support will flag as the conflict drones on and on with no resolution. An anti-war movement will grow and support for you Don will plummet---- over time. Americans in growing numbers will if they can tune out pretend there is no war going on.

Another tip Don, seek consensus and participation with allies and through the United Nations (if possible) to achieve whatever legitimacy can be achieved even though some of your nutmeg supporters believe the UN should be abolished. There is always more safety in numbers (other countries participating in an action).

In the event of a nuclear exchange all bets are off. How you're going to handle that is up to you, but, and I don't know if your mother told you, honesty (with the American people) is always the best policy, Don.

Good luck!

Oh Don, Let's Talk About Petty Revenge

4-22-2017

Oh Don, I'm not going to call you "Donald," because that's the name of a duck, and I'm not going to call you "The Donald," because in 1958 Jerry Mathers was called "The Beaver," remember the TV show Leave it to Beaver?

The Beaver? The Donald? Actually you're more like Eddie Haskell, the two-faced punk in Leave it to Beaver who was always lying and scheming but that's another story.

We can change that. I'm here to help and advise you Don.

Let's talk about your compulsion, fixation, obsession, neurosis, about always getting in the last word and always responding getting even every time you feel that you've been slighted.

Last week, you did it again Don.

Let's talk about being petty….Don.

The New England Patriots sat for a portrait with you at the White House and you got all angry that photos run in the New York Times made it seem like more football players attended a similar ceremony with former President Obama.

Don, Don, Don!

Who cares? You're the leader of the free world Don. This is a group of overgrown steroid-fed men who can barely write their own names who get paid millions of dollars to chase a ball made of pigskin, who cares, why would you even bother to waste the lifting of a finger?

You did the same thing a few months back with the photo of your inauguration. You tried to foist the lie you call an "alternative fact" that attendance at your inauguration was the biggest in history even though comparisons of photos (with Obama's inauguration) clearly show in your case a nearly empty street.

That's just common sense Don a lot of people don't like you and a lot of people are afraid of you and with good reason as you have in the past disparaged women (except those whose butts you grab) and threatened to deport others. Why should they turn out for your party?

Use your head Don. The presidency is not a popularity contest. And it's also not TV ratings.

Now listen Don! Remember Jesus? Remember his turn-the-other-cheek bit? Now that you're the president and able to melt the world into an orbiting black piece of obsidian with a press of the nuclear trigger (North Korea be warned), it's time for you to step up from the pansy who acts tough but who always gets his feelings hurt over every little thing.

Real men Don.... real men learn to endure (line from the Lee Marvin film the Professionals in fact John Wayne on his last film The Shootist said he liked being tough, but didn't want to do anything small and petty like you have Don).

You whine and complain so often Don that.........what are you a spoiled little boy?

For example, you complained in a tweet (your middle-of-the-night portal to bellyache), that media conspiracy evaluations of your first 100 days in office was unfair even though it has become a tradition for all new presidents. Perhaps because you spent your first 100 days stumbling from one disaster to the next and failure to deliver as promised (new health care, deportations, Mexican Wall), that you're overly sensitive to this but Don......you're overly sensitive to just about everything.

If you're president you ignore it you rise above it. Don. Take a tip from W. Bush. As president he didn't read newspapers (I'm not advocating ignorance and illiteracy).

I could go on mentioning little petty incidents where you felt the need to insult or have the last word Don there are so many of these repeated again and again that it makes me wonder Don.....how did a whiner like you ever get to be president?

I can help you Don.

First, let's go from petty to worse-than-petty this is just pathetic. You said in a tweet, that recent tax demonstrations calling on you to release your secret tax forms was just a few "small organized rallies." You know this is a bald-face lie and if you had any common sense you would also know this is bound to be a lightning rod for controversy because just like the "First 100 Days" evaluation by the subversive media, presidents releasing their tax returns for the public has become a tradition-----until you came along Don.

In fairness Don I will mention that W. Bush also attempted to dismiss critics of his Iraq War policy by describing the thousands upon thousands of protestors who took to the streets as nothing more than a "Focal Group."

Some presidents lie what they don't want to admit like Nixon's "I'm not a crook."

Don look! I know you've got something to hide in your taxes. So just ignore it. When an actress voices some criticism ignore it. Don't call her a fat cow. That marks you down as a coward Don. And you've spent so much time trying to prove that you're a tough guy. Instead of a punk in a suit and tie who always takes a cheap shot and hits below the belt.

Now Don. Go to the mirror. Look at yourself and repeat after me. "I will show noble restraint, I will....." Say it 100 times Don.

Oh Don, Let's Talk About Alternate Reality

5-9-2017

Oh Don, I won't call you "Donald," because that's the name of a duck, and I won't call you "The Donald," because a little over a year ago I had never even heard of you; that's how big a star you were on that game TV show. You were just some scamming real estate punk. If someone said The Donald, I would have said, The Who?

But they're a rock band.

Unlike you "The Who" deserves their fame. But that's another story.

I'm here to advise and help you to survive your first term in office Don.

Let's talk about reality and the lack of it. A few weeks ago you said that Andrew Jackson could have prevented the Civil War despite the fact he was a southern plantation owner with slaves and had been dead for over a decade and you commented that 1828 was a "Long time ago," which is very perceptive on your part.

You also said Jackson had a "Big heart" even though he ethnically cleansed (murdered) the Cherokee people men women and children in the "Trail of Tears," which you've probably never heard of.

Never mind.

When historians said your comments were utterly wrong, idiotic, moronic, implausible, absurd, far-fetched and just flat-out stupid (you asked why the Civil War had to happen as though it was an inconvenience rather than a deadly struggle over the issue of slavery)........despite this inanity....you still had to publicly justify your asinine comments. This is another example of your belief that the truth is "Whatever I say it is."

Why do you do this? Why do your followers support you doing this?

In other words, it's not possible for you to be wrong. You're God........with orange hair.

Let me give you an example Don. Let's say you said "Up is down." We both know up is not down. You know it and your followers know it too. Up is not down Don. But let's say that you said it is. Up is in fact down.

You will say up is down Don. I say that's wrong. Up is not down. Rather than admit that up is not down Don, you insist that it is; up is down. Your followers defend you saying that up is down. Then you and your followers go after me for saying that up is not down. You and they accuse me of being a member of the liberal conspiracy, or the subversive media.

Don, are you incapable of error? Anybody who has ever studied history even a fifth grade kid wouldn't say the Civil War could have been prevented as though it were like some kind of minor decision to rake a few weeds off a vacant lot.

We can't have this Don, a president who lies and calls it an "Alternative Fact," and who turns around and says "Black is white," and whose followers defend you're saying "Black is really white," when you and I and they (supporters) know for a fact BLACK IS NOT WHITE!

If you said square is round, and I said it's not, you would say you go along with it anyway. Square is round.

Don, Don, Don! This attitude is going to get you in trouble. I'm a fair man I'm not a "Leftist" traitor like your followers like to describe anyone who disagrees with them, for Hell's sake Don; I was in the Boy Scouts!

I'm not a bad American because I disagree with you. It's my right to disagree under the Constitution. I think perhaps you and your fanatics want a one-party autocracy because you don't believe in a two-party system or the right to have opposing views.

Don! Don! Listen to me. We can't have a president who thinks and then comes right out and says, "Even if I'm wrong you go along with it." We've had presidents like that before and they're dead and gone and their trickery got them nowhere the public still found out (Watergate, Vietnam).

I don't mind disagreement. For example I know your smoke-and-mirrors alternative health plan replacing Obama Care is in reality a "less-is-more" scam (this is similar to up is down and black is white). In other words convincing the American people that placing more of them out of the reach of a doctor if they are ill is removing a subversive entitlement for losers, when in fact if you were sick or your supporters were sick and couldn't get to see a doctor......you and they would scream bloody murder.

Another way of putting the alternative up-is-down-square-is-round-black-is-white alternate health plan is "I've got mine (insurance) you don't have yours...F you loser!"

I can agree with that, to disagree with that I mean.

What I can't tolerate is a president who won't tell the truth and if he makes a mistake can't admit it was a mistake, like John F. Kennedy courageously took responsibility for the Bay of Pigs fiasco even though the plan had been started in the Eisenhower Administration.......It was Kennedy who signed off on it and gave the go-ahead.

If it had been you Don you would have called the Bay of Pigs a success and then when that proved untenable would blame Sean Spicer for it as a last refuge.

Go again to the mirror Don. Repeat after me "I'm human. I'm fallible. I make mistakes. I'm not God. I should not ask my followers to become accomplices in dishonesty by defending everything I do no matter what."

I will not for example say I'm Captain America, and then continue to insist that I am and all of you out there go along with it.

Oh Don, Let's Talk About Dictatorial Tendencies

5-18-2017

Oh Don, I won't call you Donald, because that's the name of a duck, and I won't call "The Donald," because Don, when your sycophants coined that phrase it's like they were saying "The Pope."

You're not "The Pope" Don.

He's likely to keep his job.

Don I'm here as your unofficial advisor and to advise you on how you might possibly last four years in this office, although the last few weeks it's been looking more and more dicey.

Comey Don, you fired Comey, not thinking it would be compared to Nixon firing Archibald Cox and Don, rule number one, avoid at all cost being compared to Nixon. Be compared to Reagan instead Don.

Now Don, we both know and a lot of other people know that Comey was too independent for you and what's worse, he was pursuing the investigation of you with too much vigor and so you had to get rid of him before he dropped a bombshell on you…. what it is we (myself and the rest of the country) don't know, but we can imagine.

The Russians, who love you and worked on schemes with you and worked on your election campaign, to you Don it's a vodka-wishes (not Champagne) and caviar- dreams world. You love these guys and they love you. Are you going to disclose any of it?

"Nyet!"

That means no in Russian. Don, your response to all this so far has been the, "Come in and get me copper!" response. What the bad guys in old gangster movies used to yell.

We can stonewall on that Don, don't worry about it.

Instead worry about public perception, which is growing more troubled about you with every passing day, that you are a stupid incompetent nincompoop, and Don we've got to stanch this hemorrhaging of trust somehow. It won't be easy. Everything you do seems to go sour.

For example you called Comey a "Showboat" when you fired him. Don don't you see the irony here? Don. Don. Don! You of all people calling someone else a Showboat? That's like Paul Bunyan calling Tiny Tim a "Big Oaf."

Don, Don! You're the Showboat, the biggest one since Napoleon Bonaparte.

Don, then you went and whined before an audience that "No politician has been treated as badly as me." This from a man who claimed during the past election that he was not a politician but an outsider, a man who loves mocking people, for example, imitating the motor-nerve disability of a reporter you didn't like, calling Rosie O'Donnell a fat cow, calling someone else a pig. Saying of Carly Fiorina Republican candidate during the presidential campaign, "Look at that face of hers would you vote for her?"

Don! Don! You're the "Merchant of Venom," and you're saying people are picking on you?

Don, I've got to save you from yourself. You're your own worst enemy. If I gave you some rope you'd go out and hang yourself.

Now you fired Comey, and look who took his place, Comey's former FBI boss Bob Mueller. Mueller is not going to do what we want Don. He's got an honest streak. What are we gonna do? You better leave town and visit foreign countries until the heat dies down. Then come back.

Don, you said of the appointment of Mueller, "A thorough investigation will confirm what we already know----there was no collusion between my campaign and any foreign entity."

Don! If that's the case, why didn't you keep Comey and say that? You've got nothing to hide...right? Why fire Comey which makes it look like you're trying to obstruct justice? Let any of them look at anything they want.

Come into the White House if you want. Check the silverware, look under the bed.

I don't care.

Don! Don! The more you thrash around in quicksand the faster you sink. You have to learn to swim with the quicksand.

Don what am I gonna do with you? You always claimed you had a high IQ I guess this is proof common sense and IQ are separate. Listen Don! Get out of the country. Go to Israel and mess things up there for a while until I figure out how we can handle this.

You can't fire Mueller that won't work. We need more scapegoats where's a good scapegoat when you need one?

I know a diversion. North Korea. Order a naval blockade of North Korea. That will bring the world to the brink of World War III and in the tension and chaos all this investigation stuff will disappear. Like when you said "I have the absolute right to share classified top secret information with my Russian buddies," you also have the "absolute right" to order up a war without Congress.

That's what being a Dicta.....I mean president is all about Don.

Oh Don, let's talk about Talking Down to European Pygmies

5-25-2017

Oh Don, I won't call you Donald, because that's the name of a duck, and I won't call you "The Donald," because it sounds too much like Reginald, as in Reginald Van Gleason III, the boorish mustachioed fop portrayed by Jackie Gleason.

Come of think of it, since you've been acting like a boorish rectal orifice, maybe I should call you Donald.

Now Don, your first trip to visit European leaders, you more than confirmed their worst fears about you as the kind of American many Europeans have over the years come to despise----a caricature of the rude, fat, overblown, obsessed with his own self-importance tourist who ignores the art and culture of the country he's visiting and stumbles from one to the next stupid faux pas (that word means you're a dumb sh't).

You know the kind I mean, a fat pot-bellied blow-hard slob with a canvas fishing hat purchased at Walmart and Bermuda shorts with mismatching Hawaiian shirt and tennis shoes with white socks and hairy bony exposed legs------ who saunters arrogantly along the Champs-Elysees (he loudly mispronounces it for all to hear the Chumps-Ulysses), who comes up to a Frenchman and says in a loud obnoxious voice, "Hey boy! You got a McDonald's around here boy?"

You know the kind Don. No I guess you don't. You acted this way with European leaders.

First of all you pushed that guy from Montenegro out of the way. Now I want to ask all your followers and pro-violence supporters like that A-hole running for Congress in Montana who flipped the reporter upside down because he asked a question. What would you do if some pompous egotistical lamebrain grabbed you by the arm and shoved you out of the way brushing past you like you were a sack of discarded garbage?

I don't know about you but if I were the Prime Minister of Montenegro and granted it's just a little country, I'd pull your tie hard and land a haymaker on your nose.

Now Don, I'm your unofficial advisor and I'm trying to give you advice so you can somehow survive your first term in office, and to Lon, who angrily demanded by email that I call you Mister President, I told Lon, a to-the-right-of-Genghis-Khan close-minded zealot, that I would call you Mister President if you ever did anything I respect.

That hasn't happened yet.

Anyway where were we? Oh yes. We were treating foreign heads of state as though they are your employees or even worse as naughty children.

Now Don, we know that in the past the U.S. as leader of the free world has had to take the lead in leading the world because I mean c'mon, we have a bigger army and more GNP than does Lichtenstein. And I know that means we've had to pay sometimes more than others to maintain this defense against mainly the Russians your campaign buddies----in the past. You get no argument that countries should pay their bills.

But Don, there's a huge difference between saying "NATO (North Atlantic Treaty Organization) needs to remain strong and viable and do what we need to, to work together and commit our fair share." Or saying it as you did Don, not word for word, but in intent, "Okay you no-good sonsofbitches you leaches you deadbeats either crap or get off the pot or I'll shut down the whole Goddamn shi-bang!"

Don Don Don!

Collective security is what it is--- "Collective." To be collective you need participation. You might be able to get away with treating your employees in Trump Tower like that, "When I say jump you jump, I made you who you are, if you don't like it you can waltz your ass right out of here there are plenty of other losers I can get to take your place."

You can do that with an employee, but with Angela Merkel?

To use a parlance it (ain't) gonna work Don.

Don Don how can I make you a reasonable president instead of what your fellow Republican John Boehner called you, "A complete disaster?" Don you're the Hurricane Katrina of presidents.

Don, copy John F. Kennedy. Remember how Kennedy traveled to Berlin and visited the Berlin Wall and called all free men in the world Berliners? Thousands of people cheered. It was inspiring, uplifting, it made people want to be free and support the right things. It developed collective security and Don we know that Putin your buddy in the Kremlin has been acting more aggressively the past few years.

Kennedy didn't talk down to Berliners or tell them "Listen you bunch of Kraut-Heads………"

And Don, look at how the Pope looked at you, like he smelled something bad.

Now Don, go again to the mirror. Repeat after me, "I will attempt to act as a leader, not a detractor, I will try and become charming, not a cad, I will dignify this office, not wipe my arse with it."

Repeat it 300 times Don.

Oh Don, Global Warming? Eat Some Coal

6-3-2017

Oh Don, I won't call you "Donald," because that's the name of a duck, and I won't call you "The Donald;"

because that rhymes a little too much with Ronald McDonald.

In fact you are a bit like a clown who eats junk food Don.

When you withdrew the U.S. from the Paris Climate Agreement last week, instead you want us all to breathe junk air.

You said you care about the environment. There is no substantiated proof of that when your entire life has been dedicated to paving over ground to amass a fortune and you are in reality a two-legged walking monument to dirtying the air from the proceeds of your developments.

I'm not against developments per see Don, but c'mon! John Muir cared about the environment.

You?

That's like saying Jack The Ripper cared about prostitutes in London.

That's like saying Al Capone cared about crime rates in Chicago.

I mean get a grip!

I'm here to advise you as your unofficial advisor who you never listen to which is going to cost you dearly in 2020 if you last that long. Listen to me Don! Intelligence, your kind of intelligence, the ability to scheme deals, and common sense, are two different things. I represent the conscience you so far have been incapable of discovering, and the restraint that is always beyond your titanic ego.

Just like the ship Titanic it can sink you too.

In an attempt to be clever despite yourself, in affirming running away from the climate change pact, you said you represent Pittsburg and not Paris. If that's the case why don't you visit Pittsburg? Skip traveling around the world at taxpayer expense and save us all some money will you Don? That's an example of common sense.

Don, your version of Republicanism which is the new "Know-Nothing Party" doesn't want to acknowledge the global impact of burning fossil fuel. In the good old days only Americans destroyed the planet and the Chinese knew their place in your mind as coolies and rode bicycles---the temperature only went up a few degrees each year.

Now you and your followers have a real problem with truth that is inconvenient to you and the fact that global warming has set records each year for the past 10 years or so documented by scientists and their to you Goddamned science! Science is not good for jobs Don you and I know this, coal-dependency jobs that is.

It's so much easier to not bother to seek alternative cleaner power sources.

It's so much easier to live like there's no tomorrow and pollute the air and ignore alternative clean energies when we can just continue to rely on coal supplies dirty burning the same way the natives on Easter Island ignored chopping all their trees down----until they were all gone.

Then they had to migrate, after killing each other, because Easter Island couldn't sustain them any longer. The animals that liked the trees were gone too. Today Easter is an empty Island with some rock statues the tree-felling morons left behind.

Now Don, you and your followers will no doubt say if you read this, "You're full of sh't...Easter is a holiday with a rabbit and some eggs. It isn't named after an island."

Don that's how stupid you are.

You've never heard of Easter Island and even if you did you wouldn't learn from it. Maybe I can help. The air is like those trees Don. The earth will heat up and you will continue to ignore it and shove it off onto future generations unborn to deal with. By then it will be too late. Portions of the earth will turn into desert and more and more people will crowd into the habitable places left and like on Easter Island, they'll start killing and fighting over what's left.

Methane gas escaping from the melting polar icecaps will cause problems you can't even imagine and I won't attempt to explain it to you because you'll refuse to try and understand it.

In the end the nuclear mushrooms will pop and the problem will be solved.

You won't care because you and your followers will be dead and even if the few survivors if they've heard of you at all curse your name, for not only having done nothing to face the reality---but trading the very air we breathe for a good jobs report based on caveman-style fossil fuels burning---you won't care.

That's the problem. You should care. Instead you promise to make a better (climate) deal in the future knowing that nothing will get done. That's if you're still in the White House in four years.

In so many ways Don you're trying to turn the clock back to 1958.

Don, when you were in Europe you didn't go to Switzerland where that little village is where the villagers can show you a spot where a 50-foot glacier used to stand just 40 years ago and now it's a clump of grass. Europeans in this village know it because they can see it with their own eyes (those who remember the glacier).

This isn't the "Sky is falling this is real."

You and your buddies can ignore it in your concrete bunkers. You can say it happened before in prehistory before records were kept rising temperatures it's a natural event that's what happened to dinosaurs and we don't have to do anything. Don! Don! That was before a billion car tail pipes mostly in this the greatest polluter of all-time the U.S. and its Frankenstein creation the modern Chinese fascist state.

You would like to rule like the Chinese, right Don?

You see Don, facing the truth is a problem because with your ego the truth is whatever you decide it is, and we all have to suffer in the end because some jackass who voted for you wanted to turn his back on basic integrity.

Now Don. We've reached that stage in "Oh Don" we reach every week. Go to the mirror. Repeat after me, "I will seek a consensus from scientists; I will not trust I know best what I don't know. I have no background, knowledge, training to make an informed choice on this issue, and I have no life skills to consider the possibility I might be wrong."

Repeat it 300 times Don!

Oh Don, Let's Talk About the Law of Diminishing Returns

6-11-2017

Oh Don, I won't call you Donald, because that's the name of a duck, and I won't call you The Donald, because in the really old old days they used to call kings names like that, "Charles the Hammer" (France), "Otto The Feeble," (Saxony) and "Egbert The Flatulent," (Poland). It's clear from your behavior Don that you think you're a king.

You are not Don.

Don let's talk today about the Law of Diminishing Returns, and since I don't think you understand it Don, as your unofficial advisor who is attempting to help you save your presidency by saving you from yourself, I will explain it to you.

The Law of Diminishing Returns Don is where you repeat the same things over and over again to achieve a desired result, but with the repeating over and over again, the desired result gets less and less. Think of it like an hour glass where sand is running down through the narrow middle and time is running out.

 Let's talk about lying Don.

You lie just about all the time about everything Don and then you lie that you don't lie. For example for years you said Obama was born in Kenya and then a few months ago when you finally admitted this was a lie no one called you on it. You lied that your inauguration crowd was the biggest in history and when this was shown to be a lie as usual people let you get away with it.

The list of your lies is endless.

Don! Don! You lie out of both sides of your mouth and if you ever caught yourself telling the truth, you'd lie just to keep your hand in it. But once again Don, remember the Law of Diminishing Returns. The more you do something over time that is wrong, the more and more people catch on.

Let's take Comey, Don. Last week for the first time your fired FBI chief, a top official, in a hearing to discuss your Russian campaign workers, called you flat-out a liar. What did you do Don? What do you always do Don? You called Comey a liar back. Don, you always repeat whatever anybody says about you when they say something about you that you don't like. You always repeat the same word back on them---like a parrot says "Polly want a cracker."

If I said to you Don, "You're a covfefe," you're response would be, "No you're a covfefe!"

In other words like two eight-year-old children say, one kid "You are so".....the other kid "I am not!"

How imaginative of you Don. Rather than explain to the public why you are not lying you simply call Comey a liar because he called you a liar.

I've got an idea. The next time someone says something you don't like, angrily and indignantly respond with the witty rejoinder, "Oh yeah?"

Remember when someone called you a "racist" Don because one of your supporters is David Duke the Nazi and former head of the Ku Klux Klan? You angrily said back at the critic, "You're a racist!" See Don. All you can do is repeat what you've heard.

Instead of monkey see monkey do.....it's monkey hear monkey repeat.

Of the two of you, you or Comey, who should people believe Don?

Comey, who has served two former presidents and who is generally respected on both sides of the political isle (until the recent flap over Hillary Clinton's emails), or you Don, a proven serial liar who lies as a matter of standard operating procedure and who lies in governmental proceedings like back when you were cutting business deals, ruthlessly, cold-bloodedly, secretly, dishonestly.

Your fanatic supporters don't' care they admire chicanery not integrity.

No one has acted guiltier than you and the latest Don is that you refuse to reveal if there are tapes of conversations you had with Comey, and if so, whether you will turn them over so we can all hear them? If you do we will find out what many of us already know-----you're a liar, perhaps an even bigger liar than Richard Nixon.

You are perhaps the first politico liar in American history who doesn't try to disguise his lies, but who tells whoppers based on the premise that people don't care.

But again, remember Diminishing Returns Don? As more and more people see this pattern of behavior (lying) repeated again and again they will catch on and your poll numbers will drop to the lowest since Adam and Eve.

Then once again like the parrot says "Polly" you will call the poll numbers "fake news." How long do you think you can get away with this Don?

If your poll numbers drop enough you'll become a lame duck president unable to gain consensus from political compatriots of your own party on Capitol Hill as well as opponents and the public. What happens when Republicans decide that to save their own skins to be reelected in the mid-term elections in four years they need to distance themselves from you?

They haven't so far, but the figurative ice you're walking on is thinning.

The Republican Ryan made the excuse for you that you're new to the office and inferred that you are incompetent because of inexperience, you don't know what you're doing. The other excuse is that you repeatedly say outrageous things (to Comey and others) that you literally didn't mean.... they're just figures of speech.

It's time to go to the mirror Don.

Repeat after me. "Lying is wrong, lying is wrong."

Oh Don, No One Will Call You on it, so I will

6-24-2017

Oh Don, I won't call you Donald, because that's the name of a duck, and I won't call you The Donald, because remember the movie, "The Mark of Zorro?" Zorro was a guy with two identities who wore a mask and snuck around at night and carved a Z in the chest of everybody he didn't like with a sword (in your case you'd carve a D Don).

You're just about as secretive and two-faced as Zorro was Don.

Last week you said there are no tape recordings of the conversations you had with James Comey, the former FBI chief you fired because he was investigating your Russian connections a little too ambitiously. This after weeks of speculation and your statement on June 9 when in a press briefing you refused to answer if there were tapes and told reporters, "You'll be very disappointed with the answer, I'll tell you about that sometime, maybe in the very near future."

Don! Don! I'm ashamed of you-----again. As your unofficial advisor I consider it my job to try and help you remain in office at least until your single term is up and you keep doing almost everything in your power to go down in flames.

Nobody is going to call you on this one Don and so I will.

You see Don it's like this.

You were asked a simple question from reporters, a simple, honest question that deserves yes Don….you might someday come to realize…..a simple honest answer. When you're asked a simple honest question, which is what presidents do in this job answer questions, when you're asked a simple honest question…….you provide a simple honest answer.

That's called being "Presidential" Don.

You don't understand it so I have to explain it to you. Being Presidential means you deal fairly and honestly with people Don, being Presidential means you set a good example of leadership by acting heroic, or perhaps acting magnanimous toward political opponents, treating members of the press like they have a legitimate job to do, and no Don, not scapegoating or taunting and insulting them because they sometimes write things you don't like.

Being "Presidential" means you rise above petty spite Don.

It means that even people who disagree with your policies still admire your honesty and integrity and Don, if you don't know how to be that way and your fanatic followers don't care about honesty and integrity, then you can't act Presidential Don--- because you don't know how to. What are we going to do in that case Don?

Many of us will continue wishing that the president of France was the president here instead of you Don.

You must have had a reason for not answering a simple honest question from reporters (are there Comey tapes)? But what is it? What could possibly be the reason for prolonging uncertainty and speculation and fueling a developing potential scandal instead of putting it to rest immediately by the truth?

What advantage is there Don to acting guilty like you always do, firing Comey, thinking of firing his successor Bob Mueller, who is apparently investigating your involvement with the Russians when Comey wasn't investigating you personally Don. You shouldn't have fired Comey Don because he wasn't investigating you. But Mueller perhaps is. You caused your own investigation Don by firing Comey.

Why do you always act guilty Don?

There are only a few possibilities Don why you refused to answer the tape question and now say there are no Comey tapes.

1. You enjoy lying so much you lie as an automatic reflex action.
2. You wanted to intimidate either the reporters or Comey, you were doing it as you said to keep Comey from telling lies during his congressional questioning despite Comey's far better record of past honesty than yours' Don.
3. You enjoy provoking and continuing turmoil because it keeps everybody off balance and it's a way to get petty revenge on reporters, opponents, whoever.
4. You're out of your mind and belong in a mental home with a straightjacket on.

We'll have to go with number 2 as the most likely.

Again, given your almost total record of lying about just about everything Don, saying that you wanted to keep Comey honest by refusing to answer if there were tapes is just another form of lying, and figuratively a bit like Charles Manson accusing his jailor of being "callous."

The point is Don…….once again……..as almost always……..you lied……..to myself and the American people. Rather than give an honest answer you chose to be deceitful to play a political game on Comey, a psychological game of cat and mouse. Comey didn't lie, he called you a liar, which you are. Remember when you told the American people your inauguration was the biggest crowd in history and your speeches attracted more spectators than the singer Beyoncé?

Lies Don! Lies! Lies! More lies!

You can't be trusted Don.

Now, as in each week, go to the mirror Don. Now repeat again after me, "I will not lie, lying is wrong, I will not play dishonest psycho games with the American people. If asked a simple question I will give a simple honest answer and not base the answer or stonewall it based on political gain."

Now repeat that 300 times Don.

Oh Don, Let's Talk About Being a Fighter—
Fighting Women

6-30-2017

Oh Don, I won't call you Donald, because that's the name of a duck, and I won't call you "The Donald," because it sounds somehow like "The Squabble," and that's what your presidency is becoming Don, the "Presidency of the Squabble."

Now Don, you spend all your time as president insulting people you don't like because you feel they have insulted you, and particularly women Don. Don, you are a fighter of mostly women.

Your fanatic followers describe you as a "fighter."

Your new mouthpiece Huckabee set her jaw and clenched her teeth pugnaciously and said you have a right to as she put it, "fight back," in what is no doubt an eye-for-an-eye mentality instead of the Jesus turn-the-other-cheek stance.

As a result Jesus has better poll numbers than you do Don.

Don could you do me a favor? If you're going to insult a woman could you at least think up something more imaginative than just her looks? If I gave you a month do you think you could come up with something more witty and entertaining? And no Don, you and your stupid fanatics, saying "Women do it too (insult)," or "Democrats do it too," that's a two-wrongs-make-a –right- smokescreen dodge, and that's not good enough.

We're not talking about the misbehavior of women or Democrats here, we're talking about yours.

Don you're a fighter huh?

That's an interesting observation since you avoided military service and never fought in a war. You never trained as a boxer and fought in a ring with gloves. You were never a street brawler either. So how come people who like you describe you as a "fighter?"

Anybody can act like a tough guy. Anybody can brag. I've known tough guys all my life Don. It's been my experience that when the sh't hits the fan and the going gets tough....the tough guy who bragged the most is usually the first one to run....Don.

Newt Gingrich, the patriot who also never served in the military said you are a "fighter." You know Newt, the guy with the chubby cheeks who looks like a squirrel who has stored up nuts for the winter in his jowls, and who always has the smug little grin on his face?

Oh wait a minute! I said insulting someone's looks is bad.

Now Don, as your unofficial advisor, I'm trying to help you by giving you the kind of advice you never get in the White House and the kind of advice you need to get.....that from a real human being.

Let's start by sweeping away all the mythologies. You're a fighter who doesn't fight (insults are not fighting), you're an outsider from Washington who isn't because you sat in a skyscraper for much of your life in New York (living in a log cabin is being an outsider), and you are in fact a politician because you claimed you're the worst-treated politician in history------by the liberal media.

These were the reasons people voted for you. You're a fighter who isn't, a politician who wasn't, but really is, and an outsider who is really an insider, just from a different "inside" (New York).

Let's sweep away these mythologies Don. What you really are is an intolerant, thin-skinned, easily-get-your-feelings-hurt, childish, obsessive-compulsive narcissist with a gigantic inferiority complex that you try to hide by constantly going on the attack for every little slight real or imagined.

Instead of ignoring it like you should because you are supposedly better and above such nonsense.

You're also a slow learner Don. You always say women "bleed." You said it before about an anchor newswoman during the campaign Don that she had and I quote, "Blood coming out of her everywhere." Then this week you did it again. We had your "Blood coming from a facelift" remark about another TV woman personality.

I have to explain it to you because you and your followers are kind of stupid at times Don.

You see Don, women resent any statements about them bleeding, and rightfully so, because it can be construed (that word means that people think you're saying), that women are the way they are....because of certain differences between the male and female body. You see Don, I won't explain to you all the nitty gritty details, but women have periodic times of the month when their bodies change and thank God they do and thank God for women...but Don, if you mock them for it, they get mad.

You see Don, for centuries men have disparaged women (not all men but enough) on everything from job pay to basic respect because of these often misperceived bodily differences between them and us. Women know Don that they are the butt of jokes and ridicule from these differences.

They know it but you don't seem to.

Understand? Don?

You keep harping on this "blood" theme with women Don. The first time (one of many in the past) during the campaign you got away with it. This time there is more heat. One member of your own party begged "Stop, just stop, please stop!"

Now your supporters, who don't care if you went down to a bank and held it up with a gun they wouldn't care, will justify whatever you do and you'll see in the comment boxes below this piece a few of those morons and what they say.

The problem we have Don is the more you keep doing this, picking cowardly verbal fights with on-the-air women every time they criticize you is that----reasonable (you notice I use the word "reasonable") people will desert you in droves if they haven't already.

It isn't fake news Don.

You can keep doing it and suffer the consequences, or you can wise up and realize that to get anything done in office you need the respect and consensus of people other than the thirty percent who if you called them a piece of horse manure would say, "Thank you."

Now it's that time Don. Go to the mirror. Say, "It's cowardly to insult women, is that being a fighter? It's yellow-belly to comment on a woman's looks when I have orange hair. If a woman slapped my face because of something I said, should I then haul off and with all my 200 pounds behind it punch her in the nose with my fist---she insulted me after all----is that being a fighter?"

Repeat it 300 times Don.

Oh Don, it's Junior Don, Junior is the Part of the Problem

7-16-2017

Oh Don, I won't call you Donald because that's the name of a duck, and I won't call you "The Donald," because there are now unfortunately two of you in the hot seat, you and Don Jr., and last week that became red hot.

Don we've talked about lying before in this "Oh Don" column and you have steadfastly denied there was any collusion between your election campaign and the Russians and I said in an earlier piece there was a good chance this was a lie.

Now we have Don Jr. Don openly admitting to holding a secret meeting with a Russian lawyer-agent to get dirt on Hillary Clinton and Don, what did your son say when this Russian said he had the bad-goods on Hillary?

Did he say, "You're a Russian, go away, I'm not at liberty to discuss anything with a Russian?"

Did he say, "I don't care what you have we don't want my father to win that way, go away Russian, go back to the Kremlin?"

No, he didn't say either of those. He said, "I love it."

That's collusion Don. It's defined as, "Secret cooperation to cheat others."

Now because of this Don, how are you going to explain it away this time? The same way you always do. We only have two possibilities here and these are the two possibilities that you predictably use every time you lie, and every time your lie is easily exposed as a lie.

1. Claim that Democrats (Clinton) do it too.
2. Claim that everybody does it (all governments meddle in others' elections).

This is the, "Your mother if she was a decent woman told you the opposite as a boy that two wrongs don't make a right------ smokescreen dodge."

Your followers, the 30 percent, will forgive you Don. They don't care about honesty. They don't care about integrity. They will openly tell anyone this although they won't couch it exactly in that way. They won't say "I don't care about honesty." Instead they will say something like, "I don't care" (they will admit they don't care), but then add "He (meaning you Don) represents me," or something like that.

Now Don, it's only 30 percent of the people, who wouldn't care even if you held up a bank with a gun.

They have sold their souls to the devil. They have turned their backs on honesty because they are determined to believe in you no matter what. They don't have the honesty to admit there is a possibility they could be wrong about you.

I'm naive Don. I thought the American people most of them valued truth. Strictly from a majority standpoint most still do.

Don? You're going to tell the 30 percent "We're under siege" once again, blaming your troubles on the "Liberal Media," when you yourself because of your dishonesty and stupidity have given them plenty of ammunition.

You're perhaps the first president in all of U.S. history who lies and who is found to be a liar and you continue lying not as an aberration or as in Watergate to do damage control, but as standard operating everyday procedure or in other words, "Lie first, ask no questions later, keep lying, blaming others, and hope for the best."

We talked about the 30 percent of your fanatics Don who don't care about integrity. What about the other 70 percent? Check your poll numbers today. You're on the way to having lower poll approval ratings than Attila the Hun (if polls were then available) and once again you can call it "fake news" and "liberal polling."

How long can you get away with this Don? Check your poll numbers.

And what about Don Jr. Don?

What about your son-in-law Jared Kushner?

They were both in on the secret negotiations, "Let's Get the Dirt" on Hillary meeting, with the Russian and remember Don, two wrongs make a right. Everything is justified as long as you get away with it, the problem we have Don is……you're not getting away with it.

In other words the means justifies the ends, damn the torpedoes take no prisoners, I was just following orders, when you chop down a great tree you make splinters of course it's tough to be a splinter, in five years no one will care after the ruckus dies down, and a million other justifications that have been used since time immemorial- from the Iran Contra scandal to the Holocaust---to justify wrong.

 I think your son is a little more honest than you are Don. He at least weakly hinted that the fallout from this sorry episode was regretful.

What have you taught him Don?

Now Don it's that time. Once again, go to the mirror. Repeat after me, "Lying is wrong, there was Russian collusion, my own son said, "Ya Lue-blue eta" (I love it in Russian). That's collusion.

Now say it 300 times Don.

Oh Don, North Korea Don, No,
They Haven't Got Better Things to Do

7-19-2017

Oh Don, I won't call you Donald, because that's the name of a duck, and I won't call you "The Donald," because the opposite of that is "The Trump," and that's a card in a card game called "bridge," in which a player wins what's called a "trick."

Boy Don, the North Koreans must have tricked you.

Last week in response to North Korea successfully testing its first ever intercontinental ballistic missile which means that for the first time in history this particular whacko rogue state has the potential to deliver an atomic bomb on the U.S. Mainland.

You said Don, "Doesn't he (North Korean Dictator Kim-Jong-un) have anything better to do?"

This was an incredible moment even for you Don. You're always saying that you're a smart man Don. Don, where did you ever get the idea that you're a smart man?

Your money? Your fame?

Those by themselves don't prove intelligence. Clearly, IQ must not be related to common sense.

Let me explain it so you understand it Don. No, Kim Jong-un doesn't have anything better to do. What he's doing is for him the very best thing he can do, a priority, the number-one goal, an obsession, a dream come true, to turn North Korea into a nuclear power that can threaten and blackmail the world.

A country that can (and no doubt will) bring the globe to the brink of Armageddon.

If you were a tubby, ugly-looking gremlin (Kim) with a swatch of hair that looked like a partially mowed field of blackened rotted hay----a fat little gnome who up until now the world has tried to ignore as it did his father and his father before him---wouldn't you want to make the world tremble?

No, he doesn't have anything better to do.

Don, only you could trivialize with a brainless aside what will no doubt lead to World War III, the Korean Peninsula in ashes, Seoul flattened, Pyongyang vaporized. Perhaps 50 million people killed in a flash.

Only you Don.

"Doesn't he have anything better to do?"

Are you catching on yet Don?

Look, as your unofficial advisor, I have to tell you that you need to listen to my advice because I have faced North Koreans Don and you haven't, and I know how they act because I've seen them up close and Don----your particular brand of mental illness when you're not running fake films of yourself fighting in a suit and tie at a wrestling match--- is that you act like everything in the world is a slick business deal that you can lie and bluff your way through.

That's why cretins voted for you. You were going to run the country like a business even though you haven't run your businesses as good as you and your fanatics think (your personal bankruptcies). Listen Don! Listen to me.

The North Koreans Don they play hardball. This is no joke. This is no mere triviality (that means you can't dismiss it out of hand and postpone dealing with it like a hedge that needs trimming).

The nuclear bomb and the missile to deliver it to Seattle gives the North Koreans the power to be somebody important Kint----to no longer be ignored, a pariah (that means like when you call someone a loser Don).

In fairness to you Don, even though you've started off stupid showing us all you're unfit to hold the office of president, in fairness to you; the last five presidents have also failed when it comes to North Korea. They all practiced what was called "patient restraint," attempting to trust in North Korean promises to disarm which North Korea has promised over and over over the years and then reneged all the while moving ahead step by step on nuclear bomb production--------advancing deliberately---playing us for suckers while never flinching from the ultimate goal---achieving nuclear mastery.

Five past presidents tried to believe China was our friend and would help us reign in North Korea Don and gave China trade advantages and enriched the Chinese but China was never our friend Don, and they aren't today, and China will exert no influence over North Korea because Don------China and North Korea are in cahoots---they want us brought down.

Every president starting with Nixon wanted to wishfully believe otherwise.

Now we're going to pay the price Don.

Don, your followers wanted to believe you could run this country like a business even though it isn't a business and Don there's another fallacy. A president doesn't need any experience. Anybody can do it. You can do it as a former game show host.

What should we do? Threaten China with trade sanctions that will make their heads spin and if that doesn't work throw a naval blockade around North Korea. What happens next will have to happen. It's going to happen anyway sooner or later.

Or a third option, do nothing but complain.....and pray.

Now it's that time.

Go to the mirror Don. Say, "God help me."

Say it 300 times Don.

Oh Don, Let's Talk about Health Care Responsibility

7-20-2017

Oh Don, I won't call you Donald, because that's the name of a duck, and I won't call you "The Donald," because it sounds like the word "muddled," and that's what your party is on the health care fiasco.

Thanks to your lack of leadership, I've coined a new word.

"Dunelled" now means a lack of focus and a situation, further "muddled," caused by you, and named for you Don.

Don't worry Don. I'm here to help you as your unofficial advisor and I'm going to do my best to see that you survive your first term in office. But we've got to change the way you think Don and how you do business. Because, remember, you've already learned to your regret, the presidency is not like running a business.

Instead what did you do on the heath care figurative Titanic-style iceberg? As usual, you blame everybody except yourself Don. You blame Democrats. You blame Republicans. You blame the media. Like in the movie "Casablanca," it's a case of, "Round up the usual suspects."

You blame everybody except yourself.

Unlike with Harry Truman, you don't believe the buck stops with you. Anything that goes wrong is always somebody else's fault. You're unable to see Don that a president who takes responsibility for a failure even though many other people were involved in it, achieves stature and sympathy from the public, for exhibiting what you have so far lacked----courage.

I want you to show stature and courage Don instead of your always-moist petty spite and self-pity.

We're not even at the mirror yet but repeat after me Don, "Yes, the health care issue is at an impasse, and I will take my share of the blame, but we will work together on it in a bipartisan spirit of cooperation between both parties that will God willing achieve the best result for the American people."

Why can't you be more like that Don? Instead of, "It's all your fault!"

It all came down to a philosophical impasse, those in your party who don't believe "losers" should receive health care from the government, and those in your party Don who are either afraid they won't get reelected if they ban 22 million Americans from going to see a doctor when they get sick, or who genuinely (the few Republican elected officials) believe it would be immoral to do so.

I won't go into all the mindboggling percentages and mathematical equations that make up health care and how it is administered because like our tax codes, its own designers don't understand it like Dr. Frankenstein didn't understand the monster. We never do a flat tax (same for everybody) in the country or a simple (per head) single payer benefit right to see a doctor that is workable.

My simple approach on this issue is that any country that can afford to produce doomsday weapons and expand its military in the way you want to grow it Don, should be able to allow a person to see a doctor rather than die like a dog in the gutter.

Most ultra-conservatives if the truth be known have their own medical care in place and have the attitude, why should I have to pay for your care? You're a loser. Tough luck! Go off somewhere and die. But there are Republicans who are less vicious.

For once the Republican Party is a bit like the Democrat Party, a disorganized squabbling bunch of opposing viewpoints and priorities---- but for once Democrats unanimously opposed something, the repeal of Obama Care. Whatever its teething problems are, experts say the program is not likely to crash and burn as has been alleged.

It can be argued that Obama Care was too generous, but the point here is not whatever its shortcomings are, but what it will take to replace it with------ something else. Something even flawed is better than nothing. You see Don, though many Americans complain about big government, almost all Americans really love big government, though many can't bring themselves to admit it.

Attempts to throw out Social Security millions of Americans who depend on it to survive will oppose.

Cuts to Medicaid, part of the Republican repeal of Obama Care, have already proven to be an Achilles heel. You see the problem Don, is how to convince Americans that less (coverage) is better for them. Or in other words, don't get sick.

Don, you've suggested we could repeal Obama Care now and come up with something else later. That's like saying to a car mechanic "Give me just one more chance and I'll get it right."

You Don! You, the alleged great salesman, what were you doing during much of this time, the past six months when the time neared for passing the single most important promise the Republican Party has vowed for years, the single most important legislation (perhaps) during your first term in office?

Were you working tirelessly to sell the proposal? Were you speaking on the need for it all over the country so people could understand the problems with Obama Care? Were you working to develop consensus with both parties to hammer out some kind of middle-of-the-road compromise that could survive?

No Don. You were tweeting that a lady newscaster had a facelift. Or that a TV show you were formerly the host of had bad ratings. Or that an investigation into Russian election meddling wasn't. Or you were physically pushing out of the way the president of Montenegro at a European conference that produced nothing but disgust for you.

You "Dunelled" your time away Don. Now pay the price.

Go to the mirror. Repeat after me, "If I can't do this job, I will find someone else who can."

Repeat it 300 times Don.

Oh Don, Let's Talk about Grandiose Self-Pronouncements

7-27-2017

Oh Don, I won't call you Donald, because that's the name of a duck, and I won't call you "The Donald," because that's a deliberate tactic of yourself and your sycophant slaves, a ploy, self-aggrandizement if you will, designed to puff you up like a steroid-fed Christmas turkey.

That is the subject of this installment of "Oh Don."

Don, you think you're important, really important, and perhaps you are, but not nearly as important as you think you are. When you're seated on the toilet Don, what do you think of? "I'm important….I'm so important…I can't believe it."

Or, "I'm better…than you are. I'm smarter, more handsome, I'm tougher, I'm a fighter, I'm a hero, no wait a minute….I'm a saint too."

All that!

Just this week you declared yourself to be the greatest president since Abraham Lincoln okay okay you said you're second best to Lincoln and Don, is this an attempt at humility? I have no doubt you will surpass Lincoln (according only to yourself) given a few more weeks. You said you can be "More presidential" than any other with the exception of Lincoln.

That's if lying, posing, strutting around, bragging, offending and failure are acting presidential.

I've always been dubious of grand self-glorifying self-pronouncements Don.

Why stop with Lincoln Don? Let's go all the way to the top. Jesus Don, Jesus, compare yourself to Jesus. Jeff Sessions can be your Judas.

You could claim for example Don that you're able to walk on water. Your disciples, the one-third of voters who if you ordered them to eat their own excrement would do so and then thank you for it, they will believe you can actually walk on water.

They'll believe anything you say Don.

They're loyal to you and Don, that's what you need and want, loyalty; total loyalty that is unquestioningly obedient, blindly servile, hypocritically devoted, and totally immune to the truth when it's inconvenient. No Don, you don't have to prove you can walk on water; all you have to do is say you can walk on water and that's good enough. It's your word against theirs, whoever doesn't agree and Don, you're the president Don.

You're better than they are whoever they are.

Now Don, back to loyalty you see Don, you believe people should be loyal to you rather than the Constitution, personally loyal. While this is uncomfortably close to the personal loyalty oath Adolf Hitler asked his army officers to swear to him personally (instead of loyalty to the state)--- I won't call you Hitler Don you're not Hitler.

It's just that Don, last week you appeared before the Boy Scouts and told them, "A scout is trustworthy and loyal...We could use some more loyalty......."

Don! I've got to admit, it sounds like you're trying to turn the Boy Scouts into the Hitler Youth.

Now Don look!.... Scouts Don, they should be loyal to themselves, and the pursuit of truth...and decency.. not to you personally Don, or to a political philosophy. It's their freedom to choose their own values.

Truth is bipartisan Don, not party ideology.

Don, why couldn't you just tell the Boy Scouts something like, "Live good virtuous lives, clean lives, live up to your scouting creed, and have compassion for others".....something like that? Why do you always have to seek refuge in whining self-pity Don? Hinting that people are against you which some are and with good reason.

And then Don, to top it off, you told the Boy Scouts about a rich guy who bought a yacht and had a drunken orgy on the yacht (you didn't say it but hinted at it). The Boy Scouts, Don, what's going through your head? Is this something to tell Boy Scouts?

Don, I think you may have blown your cork.

I want to thank you though. You didn't tell the Boy Scouts you're Jesus. Not yet anyway.

Instead you leer at the Boy Scouts and say, "The guy on the yacht had a very interesting life" (meaning sex, drugs and rock and roll), and yes Don, your fanatics will say you didn't mean this literally, just like they always do, excusing every stupid thing you say---- or blame it on liberal media.

Don, don't attempt humor. You don't have any. Don't attempt wit. You lack it. Don't attempt charm. You're without it. It will just get you into more trouble. But Don, could you do me a favor? Could you at least once in a great while attempt to imitate…humility…. honesty….decency….humanity….Even just one of those?

Don, I'm your unofficial advisor. I'm trying to help you survive your first term. Now it's time to go to the mirror. Repeat after me:

"I must try my best not to think I'm God. I must find a way to seem..to seem…not stupid, tactless, mean-spirited, petty, unfunny, obnoxious, dishonest, a gigantic egocentric fleeing from myself, performing pomposities of poor taste that nobody on earth in their right mind could of ever believed such things could be uttered…..by someone falsely claiming to be a leader."

Repeat it 300 times Don.

Oh Don, Let's Talk About Patriotism Only from the Top

8-2-2017

Oh Don, I won't call you Donald, because that's the name of a duck, and I won't call you "The Donald," because it rhymes with "waffled," which is what you did when you had the chance to give something to your country without financial gain.

Now Don, let's talk about the irony here, and it's not just you. We've had it in the past. A president is elected who never before served even one hour in their life that was not designed to advance themselves (money and power), and then ends up commanding and speaking to groups of emergency responders about how wonderful they are.

Except for John McCain:

For example, soldiers and police and firefighters, you know the kind of person Don, people who do dangerous necessary selfless things without getting paid all that much money.

Completely the opposite of you Don:

For example Don, you recently told a group of police officers in New York to become vigilantes and get rough with alleged criminals, and you were then rebuked by police officials who said this is not the way officers are supposed to conduct police work (guilty without due process).

This came close on the heels of a speech to Boy Scouts in which for some reason perhaps a failed attempt to be clever or funny or witty, you hinted about a drunken orgy aboard a yacht.

Don, Don, these glaring examples of stupidity are embarrassing. I've told you before when in doubt to keep your big mouth shut but Don, you don't listen. Perhaps you are taking refuge in the fact that your 30 percent supporters don't care what you do. You can do anything, say anything. They don't care.

If you held up a bank they'd say "What bank?"

If you grabbed the butt of a 12-year-old girl they'd say "Nobody's perfect!"

If you ordered an invasion of Switzerland for no reason at all they'd say "Hillary would have done it too."

If you demanded that they eat their own excrement, they would.

And they would thank you for it.

Don let's get back to becoming "Hypocrite in Chief." You know, lecturing police officers on the kind of work you would never do, speaking before groups of soldiers who are serving as you never would or had. Suddenly Don, when you become president, you become patriotic---even though you never have been before---yourself. You wear an American flag on your lapel.

You strut around and make speeches about selfless public service even though you are a walking monument to selfish self-interest. As Commander in Chief you suddenly become interested in the Army, but this late-in-life imitation of patriotism is from-the-top. It's not sacrifice, not for the country Don, not if to do it you ride around in a limousine and get paid thousands of dollars.

Why didn't you serve in the military when you were 21 Don? What was the reason? Granted, there was an unpopular war going on.

Part of the time you had a medical deferment from the draft because of a bone spur in your foot (a temporary non-serious condition). Other times you had school student deferments from the draft and a high lottery number. Low number people got drafted so it was the luck of the draw in your case.

You could have enlisted and served your country but no, you were learning "Finance," in your case how to separate someone from their money, which to you was more important. Soldiers who served at the time defended with their lives your right to do this. Now remember Don you mocked Senator John McCain and said he wasn't a war hero for getting captured by the North Vietnamese and undergoing physical torture.

Don't mock someone braver than you Don unless you've been there and done that (Don you told a group of Medal of Honor winners, "I'm brave too!"

Don we have to admit it you're a slacker with an American flag on his lapel. Now all of a sudden you love the U.S. Army Don like it's a toy of yours. All of a sudden you're interested in military service.

You did serve for a time in a rich boy's military academy which you equated to real military service, but Don we both know it wasn't; it was a babysitter to get you out of your parents' hair and where you wear a toy uniform.

I know Don you have reasons for not serving. In a regular U.S. Army barracks they don't have a solid gold toilet and you have to put up with other recruits who to you are a bunch of losers and if they were like you they wouldn't be wasting their time for $125 per month (a private's pay in 1970). They'd be cutting big slick business deals and hanging out in skyscrapers in New York and wearing expensive silk designer ties and hobnobbing with big shots like George Steinbrenner of the New York Yankees.

You Don? A U.S. Army private, are you kidding me?

Now it's that time Don. Go to the mirror. Say, "Patriotism is a word misused for its own gain by non-patriotic armchair patriots; real patriotism is where you sacrifice----not for monetary or power gain. I will not tell soldiers and police and firefighters how to act, when I wanted no part of it for myself."

Repeat if 300 times Don.

Oh Don, it's War Don, That's how we Survive

8-11-2017

Oh Don, I won't call you Donald, because that's the name of a duck, and I won't call you "The Donald," because that doesn't sound like what you would call a war leader; instead we should call you, "The Don… of Destruction."

Don, you got off to a good start last week when you said you would bring fire down on North Korea's fat boy's (Kim Jong-un's) head.

Don, your blundering, blustering, off-the-cuff, insulting, taunting, childish, ignorant rhetoric with North Korea is going to blunder the world into World War III.

That's the solution, that's how you survive your first term in office Don. You see Don, even though about 100 million Americans still support you and would continue to do so even if you ordered them to eat their own feces; your first 100 days in office have been really rough.

No health care, no Mexicans paying for a wall to keep themselves out, religious-based discrimination limited, endless chaos in the White House with mass-firings and a revolving door, clouds of scandal partly over your Russian campaign workers, a new despised world view of America as a nation of cretins….and stupid statements too….telling Boy Scouts about (doing the F word) on a yacht, telling policemen to lynch suspects, telling…

I could go on.

As your unofficial advisor, I have to be blunt with you, our main problem keeping you in office is you.

But there is hope Don, North Korea. Just like the Russians got you in office, Kim Jong-un in North Korea can keep you there assuming after the war starts there's an office to go to. War Don, war, let me say it again, war!

When war happens, people's attention is diverted. Think of it Don. If there was a war, that smart-alecky sonofabitch Stephen Colbert would lose his jokes. When people are scared, they don't like jokes Don. They brand the comedian making the joke a traitor because suddenly their lives depend on the government. They don't have the luxury anymore of laughing.

Don, Don we could get even with all your critics who have made fun of you because you're so easy to make fun of.

When war happens, Don, things happen. Rights get curtailed. Martial law is declared. Curfews are imposed. Food and gas are rationed. People sit in darkened homes without electrical power shaking, afraid. Don, think of it.

You could become the dictator you always wanted to be. Remember when you called Mussolini a real cool guy, defended Saddam Hussein as an anti-terrorist and even said Kim Jong-un was a young stud? (You said this guy (Kim) doesn't play games).

Well heaven knows Don you consider Russia's Putin be to like your own uncle, Uncle Vlad.

War Don. Dictators from time immemorial have known the secret. When you've got problems, especially domestic problems; that means the sh't is hitting the fan right here at home, nothing but nothing takes attention away from it like a good war.

You can muzzle the press. Like Dub-ya-George Bush and Cheney did with Iraq/Afghanistan remember how when they mislead the country into war with that phony "weapons of mass destruction" scheme and the so-called "liberal" media never asked them for hard proof. It was only years later after thousands were killed and billions of dollars wasted that some of the public caught on that the war was a scam.

While we were wasting our time for years nation-building in the Middle East, North Korea was nuclear arming.

Don, if we have a war, criticism of you and your inability to do the right things as president evaporates, you can even under emergency powers declare criticism to be illegal and lock up your opponents------whoever they turn out to be. The lists of malefactors will of course be added to.

Don it will be like heaven, the kind of presidency you've always wanted, the ability to do and say and order anything.

Congress?

The Constitution?

 Sorry, they have to go.

They'll be a rubber stamp. It will be you and the generals, who are already filling up your evolving regime like your new Chief of Staff General Kelly. Your team is already on its way to becoming a military junta.

And supposedly led by you, a former draft dodger, that's one of the benefits of being president, you can order other people to fight and get their clothes dirty and you don't have to.

In fact Don, as a war leader, you will become potentially as great as you already a few weeks ago said you were when you compared yourself to Abraham Lincoln. Here's what we do. Have a uniform tailor-made with a big American flag and medals, it doesn't matter if you didn't earn them, remember when you told that group of veterans who had won the Medal of Honor, "I'm brave tooooo!"

You can wear a helmet and boots and get a riding crop and ride a white horse around the White House lawn. You can fire Huckabee she isn't any good as press chief anyway because now all she does when questioned about some outrageous comment you made says, "I don't know."

There won't be a press briefing because there won't be a press (evil media).

We just need a pretext Don. The North Koreans are bound to fire an errant missile that will malfunction and hit Japan by accident.

There you go Don.

No need this time to go to the mirror.

Oh Don, Let's Talk About Hate

8-15-2017

Oh Don, I won't call you Donald because that's the name of a duck, and I won't call "The Donald," because Don, even if I wanted to call you that, a ridiculous title, last week you didn't deserve to be titled in such grandiose terms.

Don, let's talk about hate.

First of all, I'm ashamed of you Don. You had a golden opportunity in the wake of the racist violence in Virginia at a gathering of Nazis and Klan members to speak out against race hate and soar in the esteem of the public.

Instead what did you do?

You made some lame excuse about how violence is a two-way street not blaming anybody or as they used to say, "It takes two to tango."

In other words, also blaming by inference the victim for the violence directed against him.

This isn't the first time you've done this Don.

Back during the election campaign for president you soft-pedalled the violence at campaign rallies by your supporters (at one rally a young black girl was pushed, shoved and heckled out of the building), by excusing the violence by saying, "They (supporters) just got carried away."

Another time you said a critic should be carried out of the meeting hall "On a stretcher."

You might say that about the Nazis and Klansmen gathered at Charlottesville, they too just got "Carried away."

The truth is Don, you love the threat of violence; otherwise you wouldn't release a bogus film of yourself trying to show off beating a newsman on the ground in a fake wrestling match. Beating people up and hitting people who disagree or protest, is big to you Don because sadly at least in the past you have been at times both a bully and a coward.

A bully will run if he starts getting his ass kicked.

Only after the pressure was turned up on you Don, after criticism mounted of you Don, did you finally do the right thing and make a public statement condemning the race hatred of ultra-right-wing groups including the Klan and Nazis. You see Don; too often you only do the right thing after you're forced to, because you finally catch on as to how bad you look.

The big question now is; what and who is going to change-------you or the office of president Don? Will you change and become more of a man Don, less petty, spiteful, morally bankrupt, or will you change the office so that this kind of behavior becomes the norm of the presidency?

In other words, lower the bar, dumb down the office of president and drain its potential for idealism and integrity.

Hate Hate! Hate Don!

Let's talk about hate, Don.

Hate is a much abused word these days and is often used way too freely.

If I criticize you or your policies your supporters will label me a "Trump hater." In truth some people hate you but most don't hate you personally, they strongly dislike you. They should instead be called most of them "Trump dislikers" instead of Trump haters.

Hate should not be used as a false label to denigrate someone who disagrees with you Don or your policies or the political beliefs of any person.

Unless they hate for real.

In other words for hate to be real hate it has to be real depending on who or what the hate is directed against. Hate directed at someone for no other reason than their skin color or religion or their ethnicity, where they originate from usually as immigrants----there's a pretty good chance if you attack such people for only those reasons---it's real hate.

Secondly Don, America is and has been a country of hate. Hate is as American as apple pie. Americans make up some of the most generous and decent people in the world, but in many ways we are no better than other people in the world. Most of us want money, love, health, acceptance, tolerance and respect, all the good things.

When some among us decide to make a scapegoat out of a group of people because of feelings of fear, anger and frustration---then you have Don what happened in Virginia.

America is partly a country of hate. The Nazis and the Klan are only a small part. Many people who won't burn a cross on someone's front lawn nevertheless consider those they despise to be lesser people. Such people are considered to be what I call "Benign haters." They claim they are not racist, but they wouldn't want their daughter to marry someone of another race.

If the truth be known, millions of these average, secret "Benign haters" voted for you Don to get even with people whose color they don't like and who feel in some way victimized by these people of color for (in their minds) taking advantage of them and the system.

That's who got you elected Don, partly, haters.

The emergence of more equality for blacks in this country has been hard for some people to understand or tolerate or reconcile. Of course, they always deny this is the case. As recently as 60 years ago a black man couldn't order a sandwich at a lunch counter. This country wiped out its American Native (Indian) population starving them into submission on reservations in what amounted to genocide we call "The Winning of the West."

America has always had plenty of hate to go around let's fess up.

It's your job Don to set a moral tone as a leader and not have to be prodded into it by mounting criticism including from your own party because you don't fully understand the nature of your job---or, because it's alien to your basic nature.

How can I put this to you gently Don?

Some of your supporters like David Duke are known hate group members and you have consistently been reluctant to disassociate yourself from them or condemn them in speech (to you it's like pulling teeth), because Don, you in the past apparently valued their support.

Don, I don't think there is anything in your character or background that will make this easy for you. You lack morality and empathy for others because you've been a schemer, a business shark, a ruthless slash-and-grab man.

Don Don! How can we change this? How can we change the compass of a man who scowls all the time in order to look tough, who brags about violence on others and who in the past has considered violence a way to deal with troublesome people---a person who wittingly or otherwise feeds the intolerance of a portion of his own support base.

Then under fire finally owns up and makes a concession.

It gives rise to the old saying Don, "You stand up to a bully and they back off."

Go to the mirror Don. Say, "Hate is wrong, I will set a moral tone for this country and step up and become a leader and not do so belatedly after the fact just because the heat is turned up on me."

Repeat it 300 times Don.

Oh Don, Let's Talk About Nazis and "Fine People"

8-17-2017

Oh Don, I won't call you Donald because that's the name of a duck, and I won't call you "The Donald," because Don, after your presidency-crippling statements on race relations this week and for the first time a more general consensus that you should be removed from office----perhaps I should call you "The Fuhrer."

Don you said that the Charlottesville, Virginia mob where a young girl who was protesting a rally of Nazis and members of the Ku Klux Klan was killed contained many "Fine People" too. Naturally these "Fine" people had no problem participating in a demonstration next to men in white sheets and other men carrying swastika flags.

You'd think these "Fine" people would feel uncomfortable and seek to distance themselves a little from the executioners.

Justin Moore, the head of the KKK in North Carolina, said he was glad protester Heather Heyer was killed and other protesters injured in the incident. Can you imagine an inquisitor (hater) named Justin? Maybe he's the first YUPPIE Grand Dragon of the Klan.

It's good to know the younger generation continues the tradition by seeing the light (cross burning on your front lawn).

Don! Don! You showed in this disgrace a total lack of moral compass, first trying to lump the victims of the attack as no different than the perpetrators, then under mounting pressure from public criticism finally two days later calling the villains (a few of them) bad, in what was one of the most half-hearted, disingenuous statements, as though it literally had to be dragged from your mouth, or coughed up after a big swallow--- saying what you felt you were (under pressure) required to say.

Then a day later you regained your customary arrogance and said again that the victims brought on their own (apparently justified) victimization.

Don! As your unofficial advisor I have been trying to save your presidency by asking you to change and become a decent man, but Don, you're making my job really hard. After this gaff for the first time a large group of people are asking for Amendment 25 the never-before-used provision to be invoked and remove you from office.

We're in big trouble Don. What are we going to do? I know, publish a list of fine people. Don, you said there were "Fine" people in the white supremacy movement. Why not list some of them?

Here is a proposed list of "Fine" people.

Boon Magoon Watson – Boon is a hard-working guy who pays his taxes. He wants the best for his people. That means he wants the worst for others, Jews, kikes, wops, and of course coons, darkies, also including gooks, zips, hajis, Catholics and spics.

Billy Bob Ray Floyd Lee Harvey John Wayne Butler – Billy is a rural southern gas station attendant who loves the old South Confederacy because it was a time when nigg'rs and women knew their proper place. When the liberals (he calls them leftists because it sounds more sinister) started giving them stuff, that's when they got uppity. Billy loves his gun and sleeps next to it. His favorite saying is "You mess with me and I'll shoot you with an unregistered gun."

What could be more patriotic than that?

Heinrich Himmler – He wasn't at the Virginia rally but he was a doting loving father and a family man even his daughter Gudren Burwitz will tell you that.

Rip Von Mueller Strangeways – He keeps a picture of Hitler next to his bed and claimed the Holocaust never happened and was a Jewish plot to take over the world.

David Duke – He also was not present at what has been called the "Attitude Adjustment," the violence at the Virginia rally, but his spirit was present as the godfather of extremism portrayed as reasonable patriotism and defense of "White Values." One of your all-time biggest fans Don, we should make him your press chief.

Harry "Fringe Maniac" Looney Lacy – A registered sex offender, but that was in the past. Today he is an activist who wants to rid the country of crime by ridding the country of the criminals by ridding it of criminal classes who commit all the criminal acts---In other words, anyone who doesn't look like Harry.

Herman Goering – He was big, fat, jolly, and a whole lot of fun to be with and if he liked you he would give you a solid gold cigarette lighter as a souvenir, another indication he has been totally misunderstood by history.

Frank Culture and States Rights Fowler – Considers himself a reasonable man, who only criticizes leftists for everything never conservatives and who calls blacks and Hispanics the "Forces of Chaos," but only to friends who believe likewise because Frank is overall a timid man. Frank hero-worships you Don because you're teaching all those people (he refers to them as those people) a lesson, all those people who should leave the country and go back to where they came from.

Now it's time. Go to the mirror Don. Repeat after me. "I will make it clear to the public what I mean by 'Fine People.'"

Repeat it 300 times Don.

Oh Don, Let's Talk About Incoherent Speeches, Repeating Mistakes in Afghanistan, and Running Away from the Presidency by Running for President

8-25-2017

Oh Don, I won't call you Donald, because that's the name of a duck, and I won't call you "The Donald," because Don, your logic is not "The Donald," it's the "Mix-Mangled."

Now Don, every week that I write this advice to you as your unofficial advisor you give me plenty to advise you on because Don, you do so much that is wrong and your poor followers have to ignore it because they are determined to believe in you and can't bring themselves to admit that they were wrong to vote for you.

Perhaps we can change the almost certainty you won't survive your first term in office but how can I convince you Don to become-----someone else.

Let's start with your ramblings that lead some people to believe that you're a madman who belongs in a mental ward with a straightjacket on.

For example, you always say one thing and then don't stick to what you say, or in another words, say one thing and do another. Let me give you an example Don. You said before a gathering of the American Legion that America is a country yearning to as you put it, "Set aside its differences."

Okay, great!

But then you go and ruin it by blaming your favorite scapegoat the press for their reporting your remarks on racial violence in Virginia, and then launch a new tirade against members of your own party accusing them of creating a "mess" by failing to okay a debt ceiling for VA spending. You spend as much time insulting Republicans as you do the opposition.

Apparently in your supreme arrogance you believe you can do without them (Republicans).

You see Don, you have been widely criticized by not just the media but by the public for your remarks that said "many sides" were responsible for the racial violence at the white supremacy demonstration and even if there is some truth to it (anyone who will march alongside someone holding a Nazi flag is not a "fine person" as you said Don).

It was still a clumsy stupid way to say it that you said it Don.

But you can't and won't accept responsibility. Neither can your followers, who will cheer whatever you do. If you murdered someone, it's okay with them. To your followers it's a cult of personality, but they only make up 30 percent.

So you blame the media for your troubles and gaffs that you caused. Not yourself. Always blame someone else Don never yourself.

Your calls for national unity and love on the one hand are undermined by yourself. Don, a man who is divisive, insulting, narcissistic------can't be a unifier.

Some of your comments are incoherent. For example regarding China and its dealings with North Korea and the point I'm guessing you were trying to make about how you couldn't just order China to crack down on North Korea…. you said, "You have to have a certain flexibility number one, number two, from the time I took office till now, you know, it's a very exact thing, it's not like generalities. Do you want a Coke or anything?"

Don! Don! I know you are incapable of giving a memorable speech like "Four score and seven years ago," or "Ask not what your country can do for you…."

But Don, when you stick to a script Don and just read off a page something that someone else has written for you to say you're more reasonable sounding. But when you ad lib, you expose both your ignorance and pathology. That's when people call for a psychiatric evaluation of you.

Here's a solution. Don't say very much. Less is better in your case.

For example good job on Afghanistan Don and your decision continuing an endless war that has been a failure in the hopeless hope that somehow what has failed for 16 years will suddenly someday end happily. You kept the details of how you would accomplish this from the public in the best "We know best stay out of it" tradition of the Pentagon Papers........and Don.....many of your blind followers are so goddamned dumb they'll say, "What's the Pentagon Papers?"

The Enclave Plan, "What's that?" they'll ask.

Vietnam. Vietnam was a secretly conducted war that failed and the Enclave Plan was a plan for the U.S. and its ally South Vietnam to control cities in South Vietnam and let the Vietcong control the countryside.

It didn't work.

Probably neither will Afghanistan. The last invader who was successful in Afghanistan was Alexander the Great… Don.

Good luck!

One other thing Don is that whenever the heat gets turned up on you, you seek the solace of adoring crowds like that rally in Arizona last week---------as though you were still running for president. I think it's become clear Don that you are much better at running for the office of president than doing the office of president.

It's time to go to the mirror Don. Say, "I will seek psychiatric help to determine if I am capable of consistent, rational conduct in which my words match my words for the following day, and my actions mimic the behavior of a sane person."

Say it 300 times Don.

Oh Don, Maybe God Doesn't Like You

9-2-2017

Oh Don, I won't call you Donald, because that's the name of a duck, and I won't call you "The Donald," because Don, the Good Lord is referred to as "The Lord," and who do you think you are Don?

Don, perhaps we should talk about whether God likes you or not.

Now, on the face of it, why would God if God is God (I'm an agnostic personally), why would he (should we refer to God in a male masculine mode?) Why would he like or dislike an individual anyway? God, the creator of the universe, the maker of all things, the cosmos, the yin and the yang and the whole she-bang!

Would God bother to dislike you? If he did like you it can't be for money because Don, God doesn't care about money. It can't be for your game show hosting or your current job either.

The reason I'm raising this question Don is that you wanted to gut and throw out FEMA (Federal Emergency Management Agency), the federal agency that deals with national disasters. Then Hurricane Harvey devastated the Texas Coast and a new storm Irma is building up steam as I write this.

Because of this, you have to shelve your wall to keep Mexicans out of the country. There's no possible way you can justify such an expenditure--- when thousands of people lost their homes and need federal relief of the kind FEMA----the agency you hoped to scrap----deals with.

What does this say about you after the failure to pass new health care and the challenges in court throwing back your targeting of Muslims to be banned and all the rest? An administration that not only has failed at just about everything it has attempted and has so far achieved a record of next to nothing, but also one that seems to be uniquely and unluckily on the wrong side of every issue.

You deny global climate change which is feeding the storm that wrecked Texas. If it was just Harvey your idea there is no global climate change might, pardon the expression, "still hold water." But this is I think the third history-making storm unparalleled in severity in just the last 15 years.

Something's up Don.

You wanted to cut hundreds of millions of dollars from FEMA, but Harvey won't let you and the Mexican Wall has to (pardon the expression) "Go South" Don.

Let me get this straight Don. You pull America out of the global coalition of countries trying to deal with climate change because you don't want to bother with it, and you want to eliminate a federal agency that deals with disasters made worse by global climate change.

Then a hurricane happens made more severe because of global climate change and the burning of fossil fuels, and now you need the federal agency you were going to cut (FEMA), to deal with the damage caused by global climate change, and this eliminates funding for the proposed wall you wanted to keep Mexicans out of the country.

In other words unless you correct me Don if I'm wrong and I don't think I am------you're now doing the right thing despite yourself because of bad luck (hurricane happened).

Don, are you unlucky?

I know you claim to know God Don……….. but does he know you? Why does everything you try to do end up in the trash can?

The Bible says Don in a passage in "John" that "Many false prophets are gone out into the world." This might mean you Don.

In Proverbs the Bible says, "There are six things the Lord hates, seven that are an abomination to him; haughty eyes, a lying tongue, hands that shed innocent blood, a heart that devises wicked plans, feet that make haste to run to evil; a false witness who breathes out lies, and one who sows discord among brothers."

 Don, you're in trouble with six out of the seven.

Where do we go from here Don? As your unofficial advisor I'm trying to help you survive your first term in office but I can't do it unless you change who you are---become less crooked----less spiteful----less arrogant.

Under the Gerald Ford-pardon-Richard Nixon philosophy an impeachment of you would be so divisive and ruinously distracting, with the important issues we're facing today like global climate change, that like during Watergate, we must avoid it (impeachment) even if by avoiding it, it shows the president is above the law and there is a separate set of rules, one for you and another for me.

Ford pardoned Nixon and you pardoned a racist sheriff Don who twisted the law.

Now Don, I know you make weak pretensions to be a religious man but we both know you're not. Nevertheless, it's time to express contrition to the man upstairs. This might help you avoid your free-fall slide of always having everything you try to do go down the toilet (health care, FEMA discard, Mexican Wall, immigration restrictions).

Go to the mirror Don. Look in the mirror. Say "Please God, forgive me."

Say it 300 times Don.

Oh Don, Let's Talk about Disasters Saving Your Ass

9-19-2017

Oh Don, I won't call you Donald, because that's the name of a duck, and I won't call you "The Donald," because when you name-called the dictator of North Korea proving that sarcasm and insult are the only things you can do and that you can't be a statesman or a leader……..

Instead of "The Donald," I wanted to call you the nuclear, "The Boogie Man."

You called Kim Jong-un "Rocket Man" Don, an appalling way to deal with a brain-washed tyrant who lives in a tiny, Wicked Witch of the West world of unreality and who has to make a new rocket or nuke bomb test every week to call attention to himself and frighten-blackmail the world to achieve concessions------and you Don-------you trivialize what could very well turn out to be the world's first nuclear exchange since 1945 and the potential deaths of millions of people----by a meaningless, purposeless, accomplish-nothing taunt.

(Trump later after I wrote this in the U.N. threatened to totally destroy North Korea in an example of taunt-threat mentality of the same kind as Kim uses).

As though from the mind of a five year old boy. That's you Don.

Way to trivialize what could be World War III Don.

But Don, that's not the subject of this week's "Oh Don" column. Other than you're stupid endangerment of the world egging on a psychological leper (Kim), you had overall the best month of your presidency so far----or should we say the least catastrophic.

Why?

We all have to understand it was because of Hurricanes Harvey and Irma. These massive storms and their destruction of the Gulf Coast and Florida diverted attention away from you Don----from your stupid comments (Rocket Man), from your always moist spite (blasting irrelevant Hillary again), and the best part Don for the most part during the storm------Don------You kept your Grand Canyon-sized mouth shut.

That's why.

You kept quiet. No ridiculous false comments for example about how the storms were God's wrath on Mexicans, using the storms in other words to promote your obscene Mexican Wall (the cost to repair thousands of homes from federal insurance now makes the Mexican Wall more unlikely to be funded).

No stupid lies about how Democrats caused the storms by Obama failing to build levees along the Gulf Coast during his administration. No attacks on the liberal media, the new scapegoat of choice, to try and buttress your first disastrous 100 days in office (if you're the American version of Hitler, and you have been slow to repudiate your buddy David Duke of the KKK, then the liberal media are the equivalent of the new Jewish scapegoats).

Not a peep from you Don accusing the liberal media of using the storms to advance a liberal anti-Trump agenda.

I'm proud of you Don.

What happened?

Did that military general you hired (Kelly) to be chief of staff, after you insulted him and he said, "Don't ever talk to me like that again (punk)......."

Did that calm you down Don?

One thing is clear Don. As your unofficial advisor and I would like all the readers here to know that every time I post my column on your Facebook

Page Don someone erases it within a few minutes to prevent you from learning the truth. You should listen to me because I have common sense which you lack Don. I posted one column giving you advice Don and before it could be erased by someone guarding your Facebook Page…….. two Arabs------one in Pakistan-----hit the "Like" button on your Facebook Page under my posted column.

I'll say one thing is clear Don.

Now I don't want disasters. I hate disasters. I don't want to be in one and no one wants to be in one. Disasters are tragedy. No one reading this should get the wrong false impression I want a disaster.

I want everyone to be healthy, wealthy and happy and at peace. I want a world where the air is clean, the water pure, where evil people disappear and where humanity and kindness rule. Having said that however, we know that dictators have known for hundreds of years that nothing deflects attention from civil unrest in their own country…..like a war…….or some other major event.

Don, during Hurricane Harvey, you even took a parcel out to a car during the storm to a victim in his car, giving him emergency supplies-----the first volunteer work you have ever done in your life Don-----isn't it?

Don! You volunteering? Not being paid…….?

I couldn't believe my own eyes. I nearly fell out of my chair. You also pledged some of your own money (we'll see if the check clears).

This was the first time perhaps during your taking office that you didn't seem petty, spiteful, insulting, malicious, obnoxious, arrogant, deceitful; baiting, taunting, swaggering, bragging.

Here's the point Don. You do better as president when there's turmoil from something that was perhaps not caused by you…when the public's attention is diverted away from you.

 "What does all this say about me?" Ask it 300 times Don.

Oh Don, Let's Talk About Kneeling Football Players

10-3-2017

Oh Don, I won't call you Donald, because that's the name of a duck, and I won't call you "The Donald"

because--- if we're going to call you "THE," anything, it should be, "The Repeat Offender."

Don! Don! Don!

Here we go again Don. The football players Don, you took what was a small thing, six football players refusing to stand for the National Anthem, and with your big mouth turned it into something major that it didn't have to be, maybe 200 NFL players now boycotting the anthem.

Don! How many times have I told you to keep your big mouth shut when it needs to be shut?

You could just have said you disagree with players ignoring the national song and let it go at that BUT NOOOOOOO!

You had to go and call the players "Sonsofbitches" and other insulting remarks that establish you as not only not being worthy of being the president, but also incapable of learning.

Creating issues (scandals) out of non-issues is a specialty you have raised to a high art and Don as your unofficial advisor, I have told you again and again to curb this tendency you have for creating meaningless turmoil, but you just keep right on doing it don't you Don?

Let's start from the beginning, whatever your opinion is on protesting police racial profiling of black Americans and recent shootings of black Americans that happen often enough that a group was even formed called "Black Lives Matter."

Whatever your opinion on using the National Anthem as a protest, there are important issues that are far more important. Here are a few.

1. We're on the verge of a nuclear war with North Korea that will kill millions of people and pollute the world with fallout and we'll have a nuclear winter.
2. You and your party failed to pass health care reform in part because of the distraction caused by your stupid obsession with NON-ISSUE entertainments like Saturday Night Live and professional football.

Secondly Don, many people are angry the players did this but there is no law that requires you to stand at attention or salute and so it's legal to protest and I'm not threatened by it even if I don't agree with it.

Could it just be that on the real issues, the ones that are really important and not like a couple hundred football players, those issues are harder to deal with, and so could it be Don that you seek refuge in non-issues, for example making fun of Rosie O'Donnell's weight, or calling someone who irritates you a sonofabitch?

You have no proof Don that football player's mother was really a bitch.

I swear Don there are times when you act like such an idiot I can't believe what I'm hearing from you. For example after you ignored Puerto Rico and got in trouble for it and then tried to make up by devoting attention to that storm-ravaged island. You held a press conference and to attempt to justify your inaction on Puerto Rico you made these excuses:

"Puerto Rico is an island..........way out in the middle of a BIG ocean."

I already know that Don.

Duh!

"I be a prez-dent. I be a macho-man. I are a patri---otttt, now I are a billionaire."

Duh!

Now Don, to make it even worse, and remember how I say over and over when you do or say something really stupid, you are compulsive to make it worse, to dig the hole you are in even deeper.

Don, not satisfied with appearing to be a moron, you're insulting today (I haven't read the insults and I'm not going to bother), you're insulting the mayor of Puerto Rico for begging for help.

She lost everything. You've lost nothing Don. Where is the sympathy? Where is the leadership?

You're not capable of this job Don because you don't have the qualities of humanity that are necessary.

Your supporters don't care. They are several types. I don't care if you're a sonofabitch because I think sonsofbitches are cool. I don't think sonsofbitches are cool but whatever you do wrong I'll ignore because I can't admit you're wrong and I'm determined to believe what I want to believe and I'm not up to dealing with a representative form of government in which the constitutional right to disagree is tolerated. I want a dictator, I'm a racist, or I like you anyway because you make fun of uppity women and minorities (N word).

Also, social media and its Balkanizing of the U.S. allows me to believe what I want to believe and not what is.

In other words Don, if I was a supporter, if you asked me to eat sh't------I'd do it.

That's what your supporters think but Don, they're only 30 percent.

You're going to need more support especially if you keep making mountains out of molehills by wasting your time mocking and insulting, the only things seemingly you are capable of, fixating as if possessed on non-issues like television ratings, sports athletes, and news media------------

-and for all of it you lack one major achievement that is unlike the other stuff---important!

Especially if Mueller comes out with that report that shows you and your Russian campaign workers all toasted your presidential victory with vodka.

Now Don, here's what we do. I want you to start practicing imitating a president-----a good president not Nixon or James Buchanan (wanted to let the South secede). How about FDR, Franklin Roosevelt. Get copies of his films and study how he acted and spoke.

Did FDR call his opponents a bunch of mother- (the F word)-ers? No! He made a charming joke about his little dog Fala. It got everybody laughing and endeared FDR to millions of people. Why can't you do that Don?

Ridiculing the mayor of Puerto Rico after this tragedy?

Are you out of your mind Don?

Go to the mirror. Say, "Despite myself I will try to act like a worthy human being with a human heart."

Repeat it 300 times Don.

Oh Don, It's Logical, it's Logical

10-14-2017

Oh Don, I won't call you Donald, because that's the name of a duck, and I won't call you "The Donald,"

because Don, the way you defy logic, you should instead be called "The Kooky."

For example Don you said you talked to the president of the Virgin Islands, and there is no president of the Virgin Islands, Don you are the president of the Virgin Islands, and you don't seem to know that.

Then Don you challenged Tillerson to an IQ contest because Tillerson called you a "Moron" after the State Dept. said Tillerson didn't call you a moron, and so what we have here Don is a case of getting angry at a lie that wasn't a lie and that was the lie.

It could only happen during your presidency Don and the way it's been going it will likely be brief---unless you change.

I'm here to help you as your unofficial advisor Don.

Let's talk about health care Don. Again.

And as I mentioned above, let's use logic. I have no doubt Don that you have as you claim a high IQ. The problem is, such a test does not determine leadership ability which also depends on both common sense and integrity---both of which you currently lack.

Or to put it another way, it's possible you can have a high IQ and still be a stupid bastard.

Let me demonstrate. If I have a pipe that won't drain-----I don't search for someone to fix it who has never in their life worked on plumbing before. If my car won't start, I don't search for someone to fix it whom has never seen the engine of a car. If I need a new roof put on my house, I don't spend hours searching for someone who has never seen a hammer to do it.

But yet we elect a president (I didn't vote for you) who has no experience in government, no past history in diplomacy, no knowledge of national defense…….. we elect for this position…….that millions of lives depend on……….a former game show host and gambling casino owner.

We tell ourselves, some of us who are stupid, that because you didn't know anything about these things before you took office, that that will make you a good president.

Can you believe this?

Do I tell a person who has never done a car repair as I hand him a wrench……it's okay, you'll be a great mechanic once you lift the hood.

No Don, No!

Who's insane here, is it me, for being appalled at your disgraceful conduct and unbelievable stupidity? You said Puerto Rico is an island in the middle of a big ocean and you want to take an IQ test?

Back to health care:

Ever since the Titanic ship hitting the iceberg-like debacle or we could call it the Battle of the Little Bighorn comedy of errors that was the Republican attempt to replace Obamacare, now Don, you are going it alone. You are using your executive power to make changes to the existing system and you don't have a concrete replacement in hand with the backing of your own party and therefore can't gain a victory-----it sort of amounts to tinkering done by a sore loser who like the kid who got his feelings hurt at the school playground------decided to end a game with the other kids because he didn't like the way it was going and take his ball and go home.

Your biggest fundamental problem Don LISTEN TO ME AND TAKE YE HEED!-----You are a spoiled eight-year-old boy in the body of a 70-year-old man.

Now back to logic. Remember I said it doesn't make sense to pick someone to work on your car who has never worked on one so why do people trust you to do successfully what you've never done before in the biggest job in the world?

Think of it Don. It's staggering the implications. You are going to decide what's best for the health care of millions of Americans----you-----a man who has no experience in health care---no knowledge of how it works----only the vaguest idea of the system-----of all the thousands of people who could at least advise you because they have worked in the health care system------they will be shut out of the process.

Instead one man without his party support will decide----on a new health plan--- that isn't.

It's Orwellian, it's incredible, it's bizarre, it's Murphy's Law, it's...it's...it's..... lunacy!........On a mass scale so huge, you can't believe it's happening.

Now, here's what we do Don. Go to the mirror. Repeat after me, "I don't know what I'm doing, I'm in trouble, I need help, I don't have experience; this is not a learn-as-you-go job, IQ is not logic and common sense and it can be undermined by arrogance. I need a Henry Kissinger who is a pragmatist and not a political ideologue or a zealot.

Please God! Send me a Henry Kissinger!"

Repeat it 300 times Don.

Oh Don, Let's Talk about Fallen Soldiers and Your Acting Like a Rectal Orifice

10-24-2017

Oh Don, I won't call you Donald because that's the name of a duck, and I won't call you "The Donald," because Don, either way here you go again, trying once again to deny who you really are.

That widow of the soldier killed in Niger, that was a fiasco for us Don, but as always you plow on ahead, denying everything, making excuses, saying you have proof you didn't say something which is a bald-faced lie because you don't have proof and you know it but you lie anyway.

As your unofficial advisor Don it's my duty to tell you that telling the truth is better than lying. This is a lesson you cannot or will not learn.

The soldier who got killed, Don, you couldn't remember his name when you called his widow to offer condolences and allegedly said, "He (fallen soldier) knew what he was getting into."

Then the next day under another one of these seemingly never-ending firestorms of criticism for making heartless, thoughtless remarks you denied you said any such thing and said you had a "lovely" conversation or some other inappropriate word to describe what is supposed to be a condolence call to a war widow; then to top it off said you had proof you didn't say "He knew what he was getting into," when there is no proof because the call was not recorded.

You knew you had no proof the media knew you had no proof your advisors know you had no proof I know you had no proof your mother would know you had no proof---everybody except you Don.

You did get a general to say how you said the right things even though he was not privy to the phone conversation. That's like a bank robber asking the Pope to testify in court he didn't rob a bank.

Don! Don! Look! You can't portray empathy for people Don because you don't know how and if the truth were known----you really hate people--- everybody except you Don.

Here's what we do Don. Since consoling the widows of battle dead is now a protocol presidents must observe and you are physically incapable of expressing sorrow I want you to appoint someone to serve in that capacity----an official "condolencer" if you will.

You can stay out of it.

In fact we could also hire someone else to deliver the State of the Union Message to avoid possible embarrassing gaffs, and someone else to deliver foreign policy statements and someone else to make pronouncements on economics, taxes, health care, veterans' benefits……

Others could speak for you. You could just wave for the camera.

We could farm out the presidency to have others do it for you like General Kelly did with your vicious condolence message to that war widow.

Don! We don't want the president of the U.S. engaging in a sadistic bluster with a woman who just lost her husband; a public debate between you and a private citizen in which it's become apparent that not only can you not admit wrong, but you lie as a defense in every situation.

A real person would apologize to that woman if there was a misunderstanding. You notice how I use the term "real person?"

Don! Don! The worst part is Don-------you're a draft dodger, a slacker. If you in fact told that woman that her husband "Knew what he was getting into," and Don, it's your word against hers' (why would she make such a thing up?)

Oh I know, she's a member of the liberal left who's against you.

Don, you yourself also knew what you were getting into with military service. That's why you avoided it like the plague.

Don it's quite a paradox that in the office of president a person has to pay honor to the military service who personally despised such service and wouldn't be caught (forgive the word) dead serving and who viewed military service if the truth be known as a no-income sucker game for losers (you told McCain you only like people who were not captured by the North Vietnamese).

If we are to survive Don I have got to shut off this flow of sewage that comes untreated from your mouth.

Let me put it another way Don. In the final climatic and most memorable scene of the 1953 movie "The Wild Ones," about a biker gang that terrorizes a small town, Marlon Brando as the biker chief is released from jail. He is sullen and says nothing to the girl who helped get him released.

"Aren't you going to thank her for what she's done?" an astonished sheriff asks.

Brando remains silent.

"It's alright," the girl tells the sheriff. "He doesn't know how."

That's you Don, a wild one who terrorizes--- who doesn't know how---- to deal with people.

Go to the mirror. Say, "I must find a way to imitate compassion."

Repeat it 300 times Don.

Oh Don, Let's Talk about You Acting More Guilty the More You Say You're not

10-30-2017

Oh Don, I won't call you Donald, because that's the name of a duck, and I won't call you "The Donald," because I should call you "The Hump Donald," because you're not over the hump, Trump.

Russian collusion, could you perhaps act any guiltier in your denials Don? I don't think it's possible. Every time the noose draws tighter you scream for an investigation of Hillary. But Don, as your unofficial advisor, I have to tell you that a defense of "The Democrats do it too" wears thin after a while----as a defense.

The Nazis tried that at the Nuremberg Trial Don, they said "The Russians did it too (murdered)." The court decided that was not an adequate defense, it didn't absolve the crimes the Nazis were guilty of.

You're using the same psychology Don.

Here we go.

Manafort your old buddy and his business chiseler Rick Gates have been charged with felony conspiracy for colluding with the Russians during the 2016 election campaign. What excuse can we make Don? Manafort? He was a long time ago. No. You used that excuse already Don.

And your, "Hillary did it too" excuse we don't know how much water that will hold. You've gone back to that well too many times.

How about the old Bill Cosby line, "The devil made me do it." No, I don't think it will work look at Cosby he's in his own troubles now.

Don, I know you always brag about how smart you are and your IQ but for some reason whenever anyone criticizes you instead of coming up with something pithy, something that might entertain or charm us with your alleged wit, instead, you always repeat what you hear.

I call this the "Monkey Hear, Monkey Repeat" syndrome.

That means if I call you a liar, you yell back in response "You're the liar!"

If I call you a phony you yell back "You're the phony!"

If I call you a racist, you yell "You're the racist!"

In addition to "Monkey Hear Monkey Repeat," this is also known as the "Fifth Grade Tit for Tat Childish I Am Not---You Are Too! I Am Not!-----You Are Too!" school of higher intellect.

We have to cure you of that and I don't know how except to recommend that you get a book of come-back insult lines and memorize them.

You said in a tweet rant that Manafort's misdeeds were as you put it, "Years ago," invoking the statute of limitations defense, which I didn't know excused the conduct of a traitor. Don, you think you would select better friends.

I want you to get a book, "How You Can Become Honest by Associating with People Who Are."

What are we going to do Don? You could try and fire Mueller and do a repeat of Nixon's Watergate Saturday Night Massacre and stop the Russian investigation------but Don-------boyoo! When it comes to acting guilty--------you reach a level of diminishing returns.

You know what that means Don? I'll explain it so even you with your high IQ can understand it.

It means when it comes to bullshi'ting people, after you do it enough, (like the boy who cried "Wolf" too many times), people start to catch on.

Now Don, the 30 percent base of supporters who if you commanded them to eat camel dung would do so, they're no problem. You could take a pee on a TV news lady and they wouldn't care because they want to believe no matter what, they don't care about integrity and never did. They think you're going to make them rich that's all that matters to them in life.

The problem we have is the other 70 percent and Republicans who will begin to distance themselves from you if the scandal continues in the Watergate tradition to grow and grow----and scandals almost always like cancer grow and grow.

Your son is trying to fund-raise from supporters telling them that the investigation looking into wrongdoing is an anti-American conspiracy and Don if you had nothing to hide you wouldn't mind it going on. You'd say in that case "Come into the White House look under the beds check the silverware take as long as you like I don't care I've done nothing wrong."

Instead what do we get from you Don?

IT'S HILLARY'S FAULT!

IT'S FAKE NEWS!

THIS HAPPENED A LONG TIME AGO!

Every performer Don knows that you have to come up with new material to perform or you go stale.

It's that time. Go to the mirror. Repeat after me, "I either have to find a more clever way to lie or start a war with North Korea to provoke a diversion that will allow me dictatorial emergency powers."

Actually Don, I have to tell you here that honesty is the best policy.

Oh Don, Let's Talk About Putin Love, and Being a Libertine Prude

11-12-2017

Oh Don, I won't call you Donald, because that's the name of a duck, and I won't call you "The Donald," because of your hypocrisy, you should instead be called DD, or "The Double-Donald." That means there are two faces to you.

Now we all know there is some hypocrisy that goes along with being president, you know Don, saying things that fly in the face of what you have done or said before, having or expressing opinions that run counter to what you have said and done before.

But the great irony is we have a president who lies consistently and who maintains the lies are not lies and that's a lie, and we have a president who has done things himself and said things himself that he says others shouldn't do or say.

In other words, Don, you're a professional liar and a hypocrite.

Now as your unofficial advisor it's my job to help you bullsh't the public, and I'm here Don to show you how you can become a better liar by being more subtle in this art, rather than the blunt force object-type liar you currently are telling whoppers that are so easily spotted as lies that you might as well tell the American people that, "Up is really down."

You see Don being president not only means you're at war with your own people (most of them not the 30 percent base), but it also means that the truth----is whatever you say it is.

Let's start with Vlad Putin the new Russian Stalin and your campaign buddy. You called Putin "Sincere." This is a high compliment for a man who has unleashed his army on Chechen, aided terrorists in the Eastern

Ukraine, bombed Syria's civilian population, been connected with the shooting down of airliners, and held sway as political opponents or critical journalists have disappeared or been killed-------in addition to thousands of the killed (above)------yes Don.

PUTIN IS SINCERE DON!

A murderer can be sincere Don.

I could say that as a cheat and a liar--------you are also sincere Don.

This is an attempt to convince the public that despite all the findings of the intelligence community in this country to the contrary, there was no Russian meddling in the U.S. election even though it's widely known there was. Remember Don how I said being president amounts to saying "Up is down?"

Here is my advice Don. Just keep lying about Putin, but could you make it a bit more subtle? Instead of calling Putin sincere for example, call him instead, "Resolved." That's a fairly accurate statement and you haven't said what he is "Resolved" about------------so it's basically a way to lie that is what Ronald Reagan used to say, "Plausibly deniable,"-----in other words------it's a lie that can't easily be proven a lie.

Let's move on regarding sexual hypocrisy.

This week you said that if the sexual allegations against Republican U.S. Senate candidate Roy Moore are true that Moore had sex with a 14-year-old girl, then Moore should resign. This from you Don, a man who said (on tape) that because he was a star, he had the right to grab a woman's vaginal portal.

You know Moore, the Alabama politician removed from the State Supreme Court for ethics violations who posed with a revolver in his hand (possibly equates pistol guns with sex or in other words happiness is a warm gun), and who has contributed his share of disgrace to the words "Representative form of government?"

You Don, who have treated women like they were pieces of meat, will tell Moore that what he did (if he did it) was wrong? Moore has apparently learned from your playbook "Just keep lying" and denies he did any such thing with a 14-year-old girl, but even if he accidentally told the truth, he will still have plenty (excuse the pun) Moore depredations to cover up.

You see Don being president means that even though you were formerly a swinger, a he-man using women for purposes of sex and lust, you now must portray yourself as "chaste," "monastic," "abstinence-prone," "honorable," or in other words, a decent man.

In other words, you Don, a libertine, a man who behaves without moral principles, is also trying to act the part of a prude, a man who is shocked by indecency.

You're attempting to ride both sides of the fence Don.

That is the great irony of the presidency. The office requires you to act in a manner that is the opposite of what your entire former life has been, lying, cheating, boasting, strutting, insulting.

No wait a minute. You're still doing all of that in office. I guess that makes you like Putin your buddy----sincere.

Once again Don we need to get better at lying rather than lie in a way that can easily be proven as a lie and once again that means using a lie that has "plausible deniability." For example instead of saying there was no Russian "collusion" in the election even though there was you could instead say there was no "collision" in the election.

It almost sounds the same as "collusion."

Let me come up with a list of words (lies) that sound good and are harder to prove as lies than the lies you are using now.

It's time. Go to the mirror. Repeat after me, "I will continue lying as long as I can get away with it because I can't admit lying I'm in too deep now and there's no turning back—just like Moore."

Oh Don, Let's Talk about Taxes and Mountains from Molehills

11-22-2017

Oh Don, I won't call you Donald, because that's the name of a duck, and I won't call you "The Donald," because Don, the way you can make something ugly-unnecessary out of nothing--- I should call you "The Bungled"----again.

Those two basketball players caught shoplifting and thrown in jail in China Don, did you have to get into an argument with the player's father after he irritated you and say you should have left them in a Chinese jail?

Way to go Don; to take something of almost no importance at all and make a taunt against a private citizen---once again----into another in an endless series of unnecessary avoidable ugly non-issues.

You never learn Don. Don, you say you're an intelligent man with a high IQ, so how come you're always doing stupid Fu'k'n things?

You do this over and over again Don, get in an argument via twitter with a private citizen, remember mocking the Gold Star parents of the dead ethnic-Arabic soldier killed defending the U.S.? You misuse the dignity and power of your office to act mean, spiteful and petty.

THE PRESIDENT IS ABOVE SUCH THINGS DON! ------But for some reason, you aren't.

A normal person with human sensibilities would ignore it and say I helped get you out of the jail in China that's the end of it I hope you appreciate it but if not that's okay it's over and done and there are much more important issues to deal with like the economy and North Korea. I will not stoop to a petty argument with the father of a basketball player.

A normal person would keep it to themselves and a smart person would keep their big mouth shut.

That's a normal person Don.

You're not normal Don.

You're not smart either. Common sense is part of being smart not just alleged IQ.

As your unofficial advisor Don, I have to tell you, you are not going to get reelected for a second term in office the way you are going. Your poll numbers have already slipped below the level of Attila the Hun and you can call it fake news all you want the way you are going unless you change YOU'RE TOAST DON.

That's if you're not impeached first after Mueller gets through with you.

Don Don Don! This is a compulsion. You just can't help doing it. Now, as I write this you're saying another athlete should be suspended for protesting the National Anthem Don Don get a grip on reality. YOU'RE SUPPOSED TO BE THE LEADER OF THE FREE WORLD, not a moralizing, puritanical busybody who spends all his time telling other people private citizens what they should think and how they should act.

Who appointed you the arbiter of all values and virtues Don?

You did.

Don the office is above it-----but you're not.

Taunting and doing put-downs is so ingrained in who you are that it's an addiction you cannot control. You always have to have the last word no matter how petty and spiteful, you always have to be one-up on non-issues, diversionary, distracting, ridiculing, personality gotcha-childish diatribes against private people maligning them for this or that (even the TV ratings of their TV show), as if that's the role of a president, when it's the right of people to think what they want to think.

I got an idea Don, why don't you make fun of the clothes people wear or make fun of the pets they have their dog for example, anyone who irritates you?

Let's ignore the real issues of importance and focus instead on personal invective launched against people I've never heard of for no good reason at all other than malice. Sound fair Don? Let me explain this to you Don so you understand.

You and I may not agree with the father of a basketball player but it's his right to have an opinion and the other athlete has a right to protest the National Anthem Don a constitutional right, as long as it's nonviolent, to protest police brutality or anything else.

What do you care about the National Anthem Don anyway? You never served in the military, you had five draft deferments; you ran away from serving, you've never had a patriotic thought in your body until now. You're a draft dodger, a slacker. When I was sitting on a hilltop in Korea; you were in a back room trying to screw someone out of their money.

Don. Don! You're not a small man...........you're tiny.

A real president wouldn't bother himself with the trivial, the mean, the meaningless, the personal and personalities.

How can I make you presidential Don, maybe a frontal lobotomy.

How about a real issue like taxes?

Your plan is the old smoke-and-mirrors Republican plan that pretends it's pro-small government cost-cutting, when it would raise budget deficits by $1.4 trillion over 10 years according to the Washington Post, oh Don I know that's just fake news. It will also cut down on charitable giving (you never liked charities anyway Don), and your tax cuts for corporations in the old Ronald Reagan scam (trickle down), style, supposing that ruthless Chinese-jobs-shipping-overseas corporations will increase worker's wages in this country is a joke.

That's if it passes, which it probably won't, adding another failure in a first term that accomplished virtually nothing.

Now it's that time. Go to the mirror Don. Repeat after me, "If I could save myself from me…….I might have a chance."

Repeat it 300 times Don.